Phillip Williams

The Failure of Human Societies

Copyright © 2016 Phillip Williams

Author's Contact Email: Canadian.Phillip@outlook.com

ISBN-13: 978-1537610825

ISBN-10: 1537610821

TABLE OF CONTENTS

Phillip Williams

INTRODUCTION

It does not matter what others do to me. It matters what I do to others. It does not matter if the world is unjust to me. It matters that I deal lovingly, and justly with others.

If you believe in a Creator, then we can suppose that the Creator placed us on this planet to pass the test of dealing lovingly with each other. Dealing lovingly with people is a challenge, particularly when one has to deal with disagreements and opposition.

Why has not the Creator placed each person on a separate planet? There is a countless number of planets in the universe to attest to God's glory. The Creator could have made them habitable and placed every person on a separate planet, which would have eliminated any conflicts. It seems that the Creator's plan is not to shield us from dealing with each other, but rather to triumph by love over adversarial desires towards one another. When I refer to "love" in this book, I do not refer to the expectation to be loved, rather to the expectation to love, even when faced with injustices.

God created everything that is good; a land that brings food for everyone, a partner for every person to love and a universe that protects their life. Humans are the ones to be blamed for forming dysfunctional societies that are failing. The land that provides shelter and food for humans still exists and the resources are abundant. It is humans social rules that made those resources unavailable for people. It is people, and not God, who created poverty and social injustice.

How could a society deny people's natural right to the food and shelter that God created to them out of the earth?

Societies employed the arts to convince people that they did not deserve their right to the food and shelter that God created for them. The expressions of arts created movies, for those who were denied access to the wealth of the earth, to portray to them the luxurious life that a few enjoy whereas they are not allowed to enjoy, in order to keep them content that perhaps one day they can take their turn in life, when they deserve it, to enjoy the food and shelter of the earth. Those who live the luxurious life in societies do not understand that their wealth is the result of taking away the chances of those who are left without shelter or food in the world. Societies prevent those who are left out of societies from having God's land to build and cultivate by themselves.

Human beings are creatures of habit. If we get into the habit of protecting ourselves from connecting with others in life, we miss out on the Creator's plan for us to live for eternity, because the reward of eternity is tied to our capacity to triumph with love over harmful desires.

The East Indian religions were built on the concepts of "cause no harm" and reincarnation, where the nature of existence is a "suffering-laden cycle of life, death, and rebirth, without beginning or end," until the soul achieves the highest level of purity in love, at which time it would not return to earth. The theory of reincarnation, whether true or false, represents humanity's desire to achieve liberty from harm by attaining purity in love.

Without love human beings will not succeed in forming just societies. It is the capacity to love even in face of injustices that can save people. If every person disputes with others, and makes claims to justice then they would angrily assume the right to defend themselves from the injustices committed by others. Anger requires military power to enforce claims for justice. Anger leads to wars and more hatred and divisions among humans. The only feasible way for human beings to continue to live peacefully together is to love even if one's expectation of a fair treatment was not met.

But what is love? Is it sensual, or something else altogether?

> *"And this is love: that we walk in obedience to his commands. As you have heard from the beginning, his command is that you walk in love." 2 John 1:6*

What are God's commands?

> *"The most important one," answered Jesus, "is this: 'Hear, O Israel: The Lord our God, the Lord is one. Love the Lord your*

God with all your heart and with all your soul and with all your
mind and with all your strength.' The second is this: 'Love your
neighbor as yourself.' There is no commandment greater than
these." Mark 12: 29-31

Love is "walking in God's commands". The most important of those commands is to love God with all one's heart, soul, mind and strength and to love one's neighbor as oneself. It is only in God's love that human beings are aligned in truth and spirit. It is only through love that humans find common ground in the search for justice and reason.

So what does it mean to love God with all one's heart, soul, mind, and strength? Let's return to the Biblical first commandment that Moses received from God.

"You shall not make for yourself an image in the form of anything
in heaven above or on the earth beneath or in the waters below.
You shall not bow down to them or worship them; for I, the Lord
your God, am a jealous God, punishing the children for the sin of
the parents to the third and fourth generation of those who hate me,
but showing love to a thousand generations of those who love me
and keep my commandments." Exodus 20:1-6

What is the meaning of "an image in the form of anything?" What is worship? What are the consequences of such worship for our modern societies? What is the relationship between terrorism, leadership, and idol worship? How to embrace life's experiences as the purpose of our placement on this planet? How to succeed in living together despite our differences? These are the concerns of this book.

THE FAILURE OF THE EDUCATION SYSTEM

The problem of leadership started from the education system that promoted emotionally and intellectually insensitive people based on their success in scoring higher grades. This led to the alienation of the majority of the population who became subjects to the abuses of those elites who secured the power and wealth but mismanaged the affairs of the society.

The elites can well comprehend popular opposition but are impervious to love and compassion, because love was not a factor in their education and the process by which they ascended up the social hierarchy.

It is through love that the world has a chance to sense and change.

Smart people do not succeed in the existing education system because they sense the fallacy of its merits. They get alienated for rejecting assimilation into that system. It is not the scientific complexity that they do not comprehend, rather it is the dullness of the actors in that system that alienates them.

Take any complex scientific subject that a child has failed in school and explain it in a different manner through presenting different applications, and you will find the child, who was originally stumped over the subject, capable of engaging with it and even enjoying it. The failure of the education system lies in the manner in which subjects are presented.

Love and care bring all people together to understand any topic.

I recently had an argument with a childhood friend who asked me why I stopped attending the Coptic Orthodox church, where I was born and served as a deacon during my early youth, when I lived in Egypt. I explained to him that since I emigrated out of Egypt in 1990, Canada has become my church. He did not understand my answer. I explained further that I was welcomed in Canada but I was not welcomed in the church. I have never broken a law in Canada, because Canada is a fair society that does not judge people without a fair trial. But in the church people are judged and discriminated against in secret without trials, often based on the whims of the priests. The Coptic Church has a strong culture of confession to priests. A person who does not secure the favor of a priest is not welcomed in the church culture. In the Coptic church a person is often asked to identify himself by their "father in confession." The church is a tightly knit political institution in which people are not recognized without their relationship to a confession priest. Judgements are passed in secret among the clergy. I was welcomed and respected in Canada because I honored all of Canada's laws but I was not welcomed nor loved in the Coptic church because I never accepted the concept of having a "father in confession." Therefore, Canada is my church. It is where I found love and respect, got married, and felt welcomed. Canada does not discriminate against people based on their beliefs, whereas the church does.

Let me clarify here that this is only my view of Canada; it is not how Canada defines itself. Canada defines itself as multicultural society where the Church is totally separate from the State. Canada does not have any official religion. Yet for me I would rather be a member of Canada than a member of any organized religion, because all that I would need from an organized religion is already in Canada.

I challenged my childhood friend, *"How can you tell who are the true followers of Christ?"*

> *"A new command I give you: Love one another. As I have loved you, so you must love one another. By this everyone will know that you are my disciples, if you love one another." John 13:34-35*

The true followers of Christ are those who love one another. Based on that rule, Canada is qualified to be a Church of Christ because it loves everyone without discrimination, whereas the Coptic church would only love those who have a relationship to a "father in confession." I take communion every time I take lunch with any person who believes in the Canadian values of human rights.

> *"Again, truly I tell you that if two of you on earth agree about anything they ask for, it will be done for them by my Father in heaven. For where two or three gather in my name, there am I*

with them." John 18:19-20

I find the Canadian experiment in building an inclusive society to be far more worthy than the experiment of the Coptic Orthodox church. Therefore, Canada is my Church of Christ, while the Coptic Orthodox church is a political institution that excludes people from Christ's love. A Church of Christ is a community where people feel loved and respected.

This response did not seem plausible to my childhood friend because it did not comply with the Church doctrines. He was raised to believe that God only existed within the Church. This was an example of an educational system that raised elites in the Egyptian society who alienated its population because they could not comprehend an argument that ran against the rules they learned in their childhood. Only love can penetrate through their misunderstandings.

Intellectual arguments do not work with the existing class of elites, that were the outcome of this failed education system, because they are impervious to sensing love.

Wars will continue because the population in every country do not perceive the elites as representatives of their needs. The counties of the Third World are in constant turmoil for the past few centuries. The problem of elites mismanagement of their affairs is compounded by the intervention of international forces. The problem has not been solved by all attempts of arguments or even revolutions. Why? People are not paying attention that the education system, that they have accepted its existence, created this situation.

Only love can rehabilitate the education system that produced this class of elites who make decisions without any sensation of love and compassion towards the population whose affairs they mismanage. Love also can rehabilitate a population that lived under abuse and learned to propagate abuse. It is not only the elites who propagate the cycle of social abuses but also the common people who fail to triumph over social abuses by love. If someone falsely calls you "stupid" or a "terrorist" and you react in a stupid or violent manner, then you offered them the proof for their false claim; but if you react lovingly and fairly then you refuted their false claim by your actions.

This education system has led to many aspects of the failures in our modern societies. What is missing in this education system?

If the education system is geared towards material incentives (money) and acquiring power within the society, then the search for the truth is suppressed under the influence of deceptive ideas (which I refer to as idols in this book).

When a population accepts one deception in society in order to gain social influence, then people suppress their memory over incidents that could lead them to refute that deception. This suppression of memory accumulates as the number of deceptions multiply. Deceptions multiply on prior deceptions. One false assumption leads to another. With every false assumption the person suppresses their memory regarding painful events in which coercion and violence enforced the deception. Many individuals would spend decades after a painful incident occurred until they remember the details and become able to deconstruct the incident to discover the deceptions to which they were subjected.

Incentives within an educational system can render it susceptible to deceptions. People want to earn the incentives at the expense of discovering a truth. What is a truth? Any subject or activity that discourages criticism is a candidate for deceptive concepts to be imposed. People in such system take pleasure in observing many people fail as they stumble over the deceptive assertions that were established. This pleasure stems from the desire to see opponents fail. Societies plagued with deceptions have high incidents of defamations. Every person is entangled in disputes with others over their perceptions of each other that are built on deceptive principles that formed rules (both written and unwritten) within the society. Incentives herd people in one direction and suppress opponents. People suppress their thoughts and emotions in order to survive among the herd until they either accept and promote the deceptive reality or manage an opportunity to emigrate out of (escape) that population.

SOCIETIES

The Artificial Experience of the Western Societies

*Every person is a different story. Do not try to read and compare
their stories to yours. Do not wish to be another person's story.
Live your own story.*

Tide: It is a sad day in our Liberal democracy that Donald
Trump was elected a president in the US.

Bullet: Why? Is not it a democracy? If 59 million voters elected
Trump then it is a triumph for democracy.

Tide: Not when the wind of racism, and every other -ism,
seems to be blowing with the support of his followers.

Bullet: The US is a constitutional democracy. The constitution
is still the same. I do not see how a republican president
would violate the constitution. The important part is
that people are being represented. The constitution and
the laws remain the same. It is good to have a change in
administration. It is like a change in the season. One
would not appreciate one season if there were no other
seasons in the year.

Tide: The election that brought Trump to the presidency was
not about change. It was about racists, misogynists,
xenophobes and homophobes crawling out of their
holes and casting votes for Trump.

Bullet: Do not you realize that you are slandering people for
their difference in political opinion?! I am surprised at
the Liberals. They slander the Republicans by damaging
accusations that are more likely to be the crimes of the
Liberals than the Republicans. Take for example, the
accusations that Trump would not concede if defeated

in elections. The reality is that the Liberal supporters are the ones who refuse to accept the result of the elections and continue to demonstrate even after Hilary has conceded defeat. Liberal followers accuse the Republicans of being hateful yet they are very intolerant towards the difference in political opinion and are disrespectful of any republican expression of opinion. The problem that I see here is the intolerance and disrespect of people for their expressing their opinions and participating in a civilized manner in elections. People are holding their political ideology and rhetoric as idols to be worshiped without any attempt at self-criticism.

Tide: I agree with you that the Democrats slandered the Republicans. That's the nature of political campaigns.

Bullet: It does not have to be that way. People can disagree on the solution but they ought to rationally examine the logic in their opponents arguments. Take for example, Trump's claim that other countries are not sending their best, as immigrants, to America, he did not lie. The current immigration and economic system makes the US citizens fail and discourages talented people from legally immigrating and succeeding in America. It is a system that allows illegal immigration. The people of the US have essentially voted for Trump to have a system that encourages successful opportunities for US citizen and by extension encourages legal immigration of talented people and to give them the economic opportunities to succeed. This has got nothing to do with racism, as the slanderous media attempted to make out of Trump's campaign. Instead it is about economic sense; make America great for its citizens so that it can offer successful opportunities for legal immigrants.

The West is an artificial experiment in which a few millions took hold of the richest lands on earth and built boundaries that separate them from the remaining billions whose societies are continuously bombarded and damaged.

There are less than 400 million living in North America on a land area that could have hosted all 7 billion of the earth's population. They enforce immigration policies and they continuously degrade the infrastructure of those living outside of those walls by military and economic domination. Therefore, the experience of the West is very calibrated and controlled. Whereas the remainder of the world is forced to deal with overpopulation, military campaigns, political interference and economic domination.

The first violation of the concepts of human rights that the Western experiment is conducting is the restriction on movement of people across borders from poor countries to the West. This is the main evidence of the control in the experiment. It is not a natural human experiment that would allow people to settle wherever they desire. It is controlled by military force and politics. There are millions of good people who daily attempt to join the Western experiment believing that it is the paradise of human rights, but they are forced to remain outside of the walls that are protected by security forces and immigration rules. Yet one cannot neglect that the West is the only place that welcomes people to immigrate. Try to immigrate to Russia, China or any other country outside of Western democracy and Australia and you would meet hostile reception.

The freedom in the Western democracy is not freedom from being experimented on; rather it is the freedom from the shackles of the irrational beliefs of the ancient world. The Western democracy is the best living habitat in the world. Every person would rather be experimented on in the West instead of dying in violence and poverty in the Third World.

Scientific discoveries allowed humankind to triumph over many of the difficulties of life that were not possible in ancient times without miracles from God. The Western experiment was enabled by the scientific revolution, but its citizens and leaders failed to make it inclusive to all those who wished to join it.

To conduct this artificial experiment, the West had to control the numbers and the characteristics of the participants. Immigration rules and border security are enforced to ensure the feasibility of the experiment. This artificial Western experiment would fail if people were allowed to move freely to live inside the Western Hemisphere. This failure would not be due to the failures in the values of human rights and democracy but due to the political decisions made to control this experiment by excluding the millions who wish to join it.

This has led to a population of hostile people who are not at peace within the experiment nor have any vision of making the world a better place; instead they conduct the experiment with selfishness and the desire for self-preservation against what they continuously portray as a barbaric world outside the Western democracy. The participants in the Western experience cannot find a place for every one of them within this artificial paradise. They compete, cheat and even do not care if they eliminate one another. They are not bound by any vision for a better future for humanity; instead they are bogged down in a struggle of the fittest to survive. They cannot accept foreign workers because there are not enough opportunities for themselves within the Western economy. The population of the Western democracy do not care for a vision of human rights and democracy for the world. They care about their wealth and survival. Ironically they end up with harming themselves because of the lack of moral vision. They harm themselves because their suppressed conscience eventually catches up with them such as material wealth cannot help.

Within the Western democracy the judicial system is excellent. However, access to the judicial system requires hundreds of thousands of dollars, which most working people do not have. Access to the judicial system is outside the reach of most of the population, which leads to the prevalence of fraud and corruption in civil matters. This drives the population to conservative politics of eliminating government because of the high prevalence of corruption and fraud. A population with high propensity for corruption and fraud does not trust a bigger body of government. They prefer to manage their affairs privately. If a person cannot privately afford the cost of the judicial system, they prefer to accept being victimized by fraud as the cost of living in North America. People are fleeing the Liberal/Democratic party politics to the Conservatives because they perceive the liberals as ivory-tower idealists who do not see the reality. Liberals/Democrats want more government and union control, whereas the reality experienced by the population is that unions/governments have managed their affairs unjustly with corruption and prevented being presented to an independent judiciary. Unions judge disputes based on political and personal whims, whereas the courts of law are impartial. The Liberals/Democrats' rhetoric of more government and union control has failed to attract the support of the population because of the high propensity for fraud and corruption.

The population would rather elect a corrupt Conservative/Republican politician who promises to reduce government, so that they can fight their own battles in the judicial system, rather than a corrupt Liberal/Democrat politician who trumpets the lofty liberal rhetoric of more government that leads to more unfair treatment. The corruption and fraud within the Western societies are driven mainly by baiting poor or lower class working people into the vices of the rich. Corporations make deals that impact working people living conditions and trade in them with money to achieve their corporate success. The society lacks vision for making every person use their talent and instead they are engaging into a competition to find fault among the innocent and inexperienced based on the elites desire to run high stakes games. People do not succeed based on their talent rather based on their capacity to understand devious schemes of greed and control. The Western societies experiment is baiting the innocent and inexperienced among its population to fail, rather than to succeed in finding ways to invest their talents in the society.

This artificial Western experiment has failed to export the values of human rights and democracy to the outside world because it does not have a vision to present to the world a recipe for success instead they are competing internally to find the faults in every person that allows them to continue on a game of elimination based on artificial unfair rules. Whenever the cultural values that work in North America are attempted in the rest of the world, they fail because they were refined for the artificial experiment of the West but do not work when applied to societies that have to deal with overpopulation and economic difficulties.

The first step towards reforming the Western democracy would be opening the borders to allow people to move freely and settle where they desire. This would challenge the existing artificial experiment and turns it to a more natural outcome of free interactions with people. The artificial experiment of the Western democracies thrives on installing concepts as idols (false concepts that lead to death); such as free enterprise which in fact is a controlled enterprise, and free competition which is reality a mask to the lack of vision for presenting a model of society that enables all people around the world to articulate in it, and human rights protection whereas in reality it violates people's natural right to move freely around the earth.

From an economic perspective the Western experiment has produced a system of middle class that controlled the means of production in a harmful manner.

People are pushing prices up without any underlying fundamentals to the economy. Real estate prices in major urban centers have skyrocketed because people are trading their homes to stay in urban jobs that do not increase production. The middle class is infested with idol worship. The entire middle class has become dependent on deceptive images (idols) of wealth that have no underlying productive value. The system propagates itself on control of the means of production without improving production to cover the needs of the growing population.

Loyalty is a buzz word emerging in the ethos of the urban middle class to enforce their idols (false images) of social hierarchy and to remind them that their success in the middle class is largely dependent on their loyalty to their hierarchy. In modernism, the buzzword was *nationalism* (patriotic sentiment towards the nation). The concept of nationalism fell out of favor and got replaced by loyalty to the hierarchy of connections. Nationalism indoctrinated the poor in the society to sacrifice themselves in wars decided upon by the elites of the society. They died to defend the nation but later discovered that their nations did not care for them. It is idol-worship that entices the elites to present "loyalty" to replace nationalism to the masses so that the elites maintain a favorable position within the society.

Colonialism appears to have been the product of elitist culture that controlled the population to rule over the world. The world is currently building an elitist culture that controls the world with an equivalent impact to the traditional military expeditions of the colonial forces.

Dysfunctions Hidden behind the Idolized Images of Societies

For every person who is left out of the economy, the society spends tremendous amount of policing and jail time when they are tempted to break the laws. The cost of keeping people employed and earning adequate for a decent living is far less than the cost of policing and jails.

Many people do not understand how money works and there is not anything that can change their nature to understand how to deal with money. They cannot articulate into the existing capitalist economy because they are not motivated by the monetary reward system. If they cannot afford it, they do not care to earn it even if it meant the loss of expressing their talent in the society.

Societies in major urban areas have become dysfunctional. People living in urban centers compete under warped economic rules that allow a few to assume the surplus value of labor among those who work under this hierarchy. Only an elite few attain the highest level of wealth, driving the cost of living to levels that make those who work for them fall into poverty. People enjoy the comfort of services available in the city, but the existing economic system deceives people into destroying this comfort through their greed to appropriate higher levels of wealth compared to their urban compatriots.

The majority of city dwellers are forced to live under a rapidly increasing cost of living, while their incomes stagnate. They survive on minimal levels of income and provide a steady stream of cheap labor to serve those who have acquired wealth. Globalization has allowed the rich to acquire additional wealth from the surplus work value of offshore employees at even lower costs, thereby driving up the cost of living for their compatriots in the same city while not employing them.

Consequently, these cities are failing. The vastly unequal distribution of wealth leads to increased levels of social animosity and recklessness, and to increasing problems of violence, poverty, drugs, crimes and sexual immorality. A CBC documentary (available for viewing at https://www.youtube.com/watch?v=KlKCBs0SyQs) explores the specific problem of women being sold for sex in Alberta, Canada. It presents a situation whereby underage girls are sold by pimps and forced to work 24 hours, as if the authorities in Canada are unable apprehend those who traffic in humans on the internet in one of the most advanced cities in Canada but are able to send high-tech airplanes to identify terrorists hiding deep in the mountains of Afghanistan. Is it credible to fail to apprehend human traffickers operating online in Canada but to succeed in apprehending terrorists hiding in the mountains of Afghanistan? Is it credible to spend billions of dollars on killing terrorists in Afghanistan and Syria but lack the funding to rescue girls in Canadian cities from the drug and sex trades?

It is not a puzzle. The financial interests that profiteer from manufacturing and selling the weapons that are used to fight terrorists are in harmony with the financial interests that operate the drug and sex trades in the inner cities of most Western countries. Let's examine the trail of evidence that supports this claim.

Who are the customers of those underage girls in Edmonton? They are not outlaws. They are law-abiding urban elites. How can a country identify terrorists hiding in mountains in Afghanistan but protect the privacy of urban elites trafficking in sex slaves? Those who are selling the weapons are of the same moral fabric as those who are trading in drugs and sex in modern cities.

This problem is prolific even in societies that have established themselves on religious laws. An Al Jazeera documentary on the slave trade (available for viewing at https://www.youtube.com/watch?v=t8CASmDNo_s) considers the example of slavery in Pakistan, a country that established itself based on Islamic religious rules that purport to enable worship of a monotheistic God. People do not adhere to the laws that are on the books. In all the countries of the world, the reality among the general population does not correspond with the political rhetoric or the laws. This documentary presents a situation of a woman who sold her kidney (which went to a rich Arab customer) in order to offset her debt.

Various documentaries examine the dysfunctions of society in modern cities, many of them available on YouTube. The topics range from children being trafficked in Africa to work for the cocoa industry that produces the chocolate enjoyed in the West, to women being trafficked in major European cities to serve in the sex trade.

An Al Jazeera documentary series on slavery includes a film on child slavery (available for viewing at https://www.youtube.com/watch?v=xVo2TabkW8I) that chronicles the situation in Haiti, a society that rose from slavery during the colonial era, only to come to abuse elements of the population through a concept called "restavek" that allows poor children to be placed under the care of richer families. This serves as evidence that slavery is not a function of racism; instead both racism and slavery are functions of idolatry (the worship of false concepts of societal wealth that appear profitable or workable but lead to spiritual death and serious dysfunction).

Another film in the series is called *Charcoal slaves* [1] and describes the situation of about one quarter of a million people in Brazil. It can be viewed at https://www.youtube.com/watch?v=dfbdqVv9tiE.

No discussion of slavery would be complete without an examination of India's social system. The documentary *Bridal Slaves* [2] can be viewed at https://www.youtube.com/watch?v=arSEALgiOr4.

In a debate that took place in Washington (the recorded version is available at https://www.youtube.com/watch?v=tz7R4qSdJB0), the participants identify slavery as characterized by the complete control of one person by another, the use of violence to maintain that control, and economic exploitation. The victims of slavery amount to 27 million in the world today.

Why would anyone attempt to control another person by violence?

People might control one another either to actively extract benefits or to passively impose a punishment.

The concept of economic benefit or pleasure derived from controlling another person is an idol worship that is deeply rooted in a cultural ethos that has not been remedied by the Industrial or Technological Revolutions.

Controlling another person or aiding the enslavement of another person as a form of punishment can be due to the same idol worship that causes people kill one another, e.g. injury to dignity or fear of demographic growth of a certain ethnic group. A tribe that is afraid of the collective force of another tribe would conspire to weaken the other tribe in order for their enemies to rule over them. The parents in some dysfunctional families wish that their disobedient or displeasing children become slaves to their siblings who are pleasing to their parents.

In this debate it is argued that slavery can be eliminated at a cost of about 20 billion dollars over a 25-year period. Why has it not happened?

Victims of modern slavery are not tied by chains of steel but rather by chains of fear. They know that if they escape their masters, there will be no one in the society that cares to help them. Their economic and social conditions will persist even if they escape because of a lack of care. Most who escape eventually return to those who control them.

Urban middle-class consumers want to see cheaper costs for convenient technology and services but do not understand where these cheap prices come from. Do they come from bonded workers (under debt with increasing interest rates) or from Chinese prisoners (making consumer goods in China)? Both are servants of a capitalist system that controls them by fear and under escalating conditions of financial debt.

In 2008 the world's middle class watched as their savings disappeared from most financial institutions and stock market investments. This event plunged millions into debt and put them into slavery of a kind. The social system did not have any remedy; instead it sanctioned this massive economic process by which millions were continuously placed under slave-like work conditions.

The Industrial and Technological Revolutions do not seem to have brought any real relief from slavery; instead they have built a façade to cover up the problems brought on by idolatry. The façade of modern societies is a deceptive tomb shining from the outside but hiding skeletons of dead bodies beneath it.

The political systems of all of our modern world cities have failed to generate plans for the living needs of every member of their populations because of the failure to graduate leaders that truly serve and represent people rather than rule over them by military and police force. Our universities graduate scientists who are more likely to be employed to build high-tech weaponry than to devise urban planning to ensure decent living standards (including jobs, education and health care) for all. Billions of dollars of tax money collected from the population are expended on military budgets instead of on planning for the living needs of the population.

It gets worse when people have negative encounters with those who are supposed to represent them. Personally I have had my share of such experiences in Canada. How many times have you contacted your government regarding a social issue that impacts you only to get an unwelcome response? How many times have you contacted your representative in Parliament or the Senate only to hear back that the representative does not want to meet you? Perhaps you have never tried because you believe that you haven't needed to. But if you sought to present your representative with an opposing political view you would likely get a cold response. Why? In reality such representatives do not represent their constituents but rather the powers that brought them to office.

If the government and the political representatives make their constituency feel unwelcome then people inevitably lose trust in the moral foundation of society.

The moral foundation of society is questioned not only when dealing with government and politicians but also when citizens deal with one another in Western countries—often in kind ways but also in cold and calculated ways.

It is the lost sense of trust in the moral fabric of Western societies that drives first- and second-generation immigrants to join terrorist organizations in the fanciful dream of establishing an Islamic State based on moral grounds.

Religious institutions all too often sanction this dysfunctional system and bless the leaders who perpetuate it, thereby violating their moral commitment to the expound the truth. This is the main reason why so many are repulsed by the various institutions of organized religion. They do not worship in truth as Jesus Christ preached. Most people who claim to be 'spiritual but not religious' do not want to be morally implicated in the crimes of the authorities—crimes that religious institutions have sanctioned if not participated in.

Societies maintain idolized images by propagandizing the positive aspects of their social structures while hiding all of their ills, thereby holding false images about their structures and the quality of their elites.

The existing institutions of societies as well as the culture of modernity are plagued with structural instability that is suppressed by the media in order to maintain a façade of success.

The world has known divisions based on the desire to identify with nationalist ideologies and religions, which are perceptive images to which the individual is exhorted to pay ultimate loyalty to the extent of sacrificing his or her life.

Religions exhort their followers to defend the faith with their lives. Nationalist ideologies exhort their followers to defend the nation with their lives. In these practices, religions and ideologies become idols accorded loyalty above one's loyalty to reason and one's conscience. Both of these idols exhort the individual to kill, thereby violating the commandment "thou shalt not kill", and placing the individual under the authority of political leadership whose wars are motivated by worship of power, money, or any idol other than reason, and certainly not God, who forbade killing. Instead the first commandment ought to have been worth identifying with because it liberates the individual from worshipping any idol.□

The world is full of deceptive ideas that have become idols. Take, for example, the lie that the earth is overpopulated whereas the fact is that a land the area of Texas could provide a home with a little personal farm or garden for every family on this planet and the remainder of the earth would be empty, as explained in this video on YouTube: https://www.youtube.com/watch?v=vZVOU5bfHrM.

This is not surprising considering that the land area of Texas is 268,800 sq. miles. If you divide that over three billion families, you get about 2,500 sq. feet (232 sq. meters) of land per family.

Take the example of the number of newborn babies with drug addiction in Canada. A CBC news article dated October 4, 2015, titled "Almost half of newborns seized in Manitoba have developmental, addiction issues" [3], explains that in Manitoba alone a newborn baby is seized by the family services ministry for developmental and addiction issues every day. This is a structural dysfunction, and not simply an aberration within a culture of one of the richest modern nations of the world.

Another news article dated October 3, 2015, titled "Vatican Fires Gay Priest Who Came Out Before Global Meeting" [4], describes dysfunction inside one of the biggest religious institutions, the Catholic Church, where a priest who had been a member of the church's doctrine office for a decade started a campaign promoting homosexuality.

Definition of the Problem and Root Cause Analysis (RCA)

The world's elites appear to be in a state of deference to figures of authority under the influence of group pressure no less pathological than that described in Hans Christian Andersen's 1837 tale *The Emperor's New Clothes*. It is a story about two weavers who promise an emperor a new suit of clothes that is invisible to those who are unfit for their position, stupid, or incompetent. The suit is imaginary. Yet people do not dare to admit that they cannot see it.

The richest one billion of the earth's population make one hundred dollars or more per day. The poorest one billion make a dollar or less per day. (See the documentary *Don't Panic* by Hans Rosling, a Swedish medical doctor, academic, statistician, and public speaker. https://www.youtube.com/watch?v=-UbmG8gtBPM [5]) The situation is unstable, with the richest one billion dreading the possibility of falling out of their income bracket and the poorest one billion unable to live with dignity.

The elites' fear of loss of social privilege propels their deference to authority that is not representative of the entire population; rather it is an authority voted for and maintained by that fear. The world's manufactured democracies are built on fear-motivated protection of the privileges of elites rather than on planning for the needs of all. It is a democracy that feeds on xenophobia and modern forms of slavery, as I will show later in the chapter.

In every country, politicians authorize massive borrowing deals in which debts are incurred on the poorest population for several generations while the benefits of those debts are reaped by the elites who rule over them. The population is not consulted before debts are incurred or before massive spending on foreign policies and military interventions are made. What do you call assigning debt to you and to your children without your permission and without benefiting from those loans?

The comfortable one billion of the earth's population do not wish to hear the voices of the remaining six billion or to see their dysfunctional social reality. Their deafness and blindness are maintained through the media's biases. Dissenting voices are ignored, silenced, or suppressed and any available resources are withdrawn from protesters. With the writer of Matthew 24, we might ask:

> *"Who then is the faithful and wise servant, whom the master has put in charge of the servants in his household to give them their food at the proper time?" Matt. 24:45*

The one billion human beings who live comfortably have installed figures of authority in their societies in order to silence the remaining six billion who are shouting that the system is not working for them. The elites are no longer viewed as successful managers of the affairs of remaining six billion and have lost their legitimacy to govern from the perspective of the general population.

The elites have convinced themselves that the protesters are either stupid and lazy or terrorists, and have concluded that the existing system need not be called into question. The media exerts tremendous effort to convince the dissenting population that their problem is of their own making. The six billion for whom the system is not working are subjugated under the rule of the law, which can be bent in favor of those in power and imprisons those who owe a penny compounded by high interest rates to a lender. Deference to the installed authority is enforced by those one billion elites toward the remaining six billion as a form of idol worship.

The elites punish the population by police and military force for their persistent complaints about this failing system. Any claim that the current system is flawed is ridiculed and suppressed. People's lives do not matter to the elites who run this system so much as their pride in assuming leadership of the suffering population. The elites build plenty of prisons for political dissenters and spend taxpayer money on weapons to kill dissenters instead of creating jobs and building schools and hospitals for the same population.

The social order is fragile. The evidence lies in the prevalence of wars and terrorism, the increase in human trafficking, whose victims constantly flee from impoverished and oppressed regions of the world to the West, and the various forms of modern slavery.

Religious institutions have entered this arena of social deception to enforce deference to authority rather than to expound the truth of the situation—namely that there are six billion people for whom this system is not working under the management of elites who have installed an idolatry of worshiping authority not only to silence any dissent but also to quell the richest one billion's fear of falling into poverty.

Idol worship has resulted in a situation in which one billion human beings are utilizing the resources of the planet to control, rather than to plan for, the remaining six billion human beings. The elites have become rulers, instead of servants, of the entire population.

The six billion who are facing marginalization react in various ways that range from peaceful to violent, and experience significant pathological symptoms. If you read the statistics on the U.S. Substance Abuse and Mental Health Services Administration (SAMHSA) (see http://www.samhsa.gov) you will learn that the number of people afflicted with mental illness in 2015 reached 43.5 million and that the number of people addicted to illicit drug usage reached 10% of the population (i.e. close to 32 million people). If these are the social realities in the most advanced country in the world, imagine how far worse they are in oppressed countries around the world that do not maintain or publish statistics pertaining to social dysfunction.

Debt, drugs, mental illness and sexual immorality are tearing apart the lives of people all around the world. The elites who insist on maintaining the current social system use statistics to show that the majority of people are incapable of governing themselves; but in reality if you seek to discover who is behind the drug and sex trades, you will find the same elites that keep this system alive. They sell weapons to people to fight in order to increase profits and claim that those people are not fit to self-govern. They sell drugs and allow sexual exploitation to claim that people are mentally ill and not capable of deciding how their lives should be run. The pervasiveness of pathological symptoms is the result of elites who do not wish to give up control of the world's resources.

Take, for example, the vast areas of uninhabited land in every country that people are not allowed to develop. Why should any group of people be prevented from living on or cultivating uninhabited land? Why aren't the public funds that the rulers of those societies spend on the weapons industry used to help communities develop uninhabited land? Instead societies cram people into urban centers. Each family or individual lives in shelters of roughly 800 to 2000 square feet that cost hundreds of thousands of dollars and are purchased on credit, with people enslaved to pay the debt for the remainder of their lives under the constant bombardment of money lenders (banks), illicit drug traders and various social dysfunctions. Is it credible to live in an era of advanced scientific discoveries that allow us to travel in outer space, yet still be bereft of a better social system?

The problem is not caused by a conspiracy that can be solved through a bloody revolution, but rather by idolatry that can only be solved through a peaceful spiritual revolution. A bloody revolution will only replace one group of immoral elites with another such group. That's not to say that the leadership did not contribute to the existing problems. Leadership contributed to these problems because the values by which people promote others to leadership position are not healthy.

We already know that political divisions and social hatred cause people to harm one another. It is unimaginable for an Islamic population to give land to Jews to live on, just as it is unimaginable for the U.S. or Israel to give land to Islamists to build an Islamic state in their communities. Similar arguments can be made of other political or religious groups—for example, Hindus in relation to Muslims, Muslims in relation to Christians, or Chinese citizens in relation to Japanese citizens.

People have learned to love their friends and neighbors and to hate, curse and fight their enemies, despite the Biblical injunction:

> *"But to you who are listening I say: Love your enemies, do good to those who hate you, bless those who curse you, pray for those who mistreat you. If someone slaps you on one cheek, turn to them the other also. If someone takes your coat, do not withhold your shirt from them. Give to everyone who asks you, and if anyone takes what belongs to you, do not demand it back."*
>
> *Luke 6: 27-30*

People of one country engage in warfare against their enemies in another country. It is unimaginable that one country would help its enemies to live a decent life on the enemy's land, let alone on their own land.

Why is humankind divided by enmity? The answer is idolatry.

People have created idols out of religious and national identities. They have created deceptive ideas to be feared and loved. People worship what they fear and love. If people love and fear the Creator then they will be loving even towards people who are hostile to them. But if they love and fear their respective religious teachings (that are often at odds with other religions), and their national identities and political leaders, then they will become enemies of one another.

The famous song "Imagine" by John Lennon, the English singer and co-founder of *The Beatles*, got it right in one aspect but wrong in another with its line, "Imagine there's no countries / It isn't hard to do / Nothing to kill or die for / And no religion too / Imagine all the people / Living life in peace." Without national and religious identities human lives would be more peaceful. But the claim that peace could exist if humans rejected the belief in an afterlife is incorrect. Belief in eternal life motivates people to react peacefully to the adversity of life on earth. Belief in eternal life and God is different from belief in the divisive idols of religious and national pride.

One might ask: How is political and religious division related to the fact that one billion of the earth's elites control the remaining six billion under unfair living conditions? The answer takes the form of another question: Once people are deceived into following divisive political and religious idols that make them enemies of one another, what reason is there to expect that they would not worship money and abuse one another to extract material gains? Do you think that the elites of one national identity, who are inciting their population to war against those with another national identity, would be less murderous towards people of shared identity? Even in our modern cities, people often lose their jobs due to difference of opinions; politics causes people within the same family to marginalize and isolate each other. Do you think that a human population so extremely divided can get together to honestly set up plans for the living needs of the entire population?

I hope you see now that the problem is not due to a conspiracy by certain elites that would be solved by a military jihad or a revolution that removes those elites and restores justice. The problem is spiritual. It is the population's fear and love of divisive idols beside the Creator. It the population's obedience to idol worship that causes them to sheepishly accept this failed system and give it undeserving lip service.

If one does not believe in eternal life and love of the Creator then one is likely to be deceived by idols of hatred, whether religious, national or economic. It is through belief in eternal life and love of the Creator that people can subdue their desire for hate-filled wars and love their political opponents.

Only with love can human beings succeed in achieving justice and in triumphing over the idols of hatred and war.

Ideological Bullet

Bullet: I wanted to love and be loved. But the Church turned our generation into ideological projectiles. The friends I met in the Church were only an ideological brotherhood. They never stayed friends for long. Judgements over religious issues, without consideration of the different circumstances of every person, turned into an unpleasant experience. The Church harmed all of us. We did not form any friendships. Instead we were driven to build the Church's political influence and judge one another based on obedience and adherence to Church doctrines.

Tide: You put yourself in a corner. You will not succeed in life. You do not develop affluent connections. Your connections are made up of losers. You believe that God will achieve things for you. But you have very little to show for this belief. If God existed, and you are honest in your belief in God, he would have helped you become a success. So either God is a form of wishful thinking, or your belief in God is not true. Churchgoers who believe in God and follow the Church would be more inclined to think that it is you who is wrong in your belief. You do not have God's holy spirit.

Bullet: It's God's will. I maintained my love towards people and sought excuses when someone made mistakes. I have sought people's friendship. I admit that sometimes the more I tried to earn friendships the more I lost them. People do not easily trust different people. I have not betrayed anyone who depended on me. Therefore, I accepted that it was God's will. Maybe I should not have cared that much to make friends with everyone.

There are people do not care for friendship.

Tide: Maybe you are just not the kind of person who gets along easily with people.

Bullet: I thought that I protected and supported those who worked with me. They often misunderstood me and sometimes turned hostile toward me for staying silent. You are right in one aspect. I did not approve of the culture of my generation and did not go along easily. I even did not approve of any organized religion I experimented with. I did not approve of the atheist rhetoric either. I did not belong to any of those cultures of my generation and did not get along easily with people who believed in them.

Tide: People with whom you worked wanted you to approve of their desire to swim against the tide but you did not. You have always been distrustful of people and extremely sensitive to their careless speech. You are as authentic in your relationships as a bullet.

Inspiration: Both of you, take it easy. Let's take a different look at things. An idea is a powerful force in our minds. Have you considered the possibility that our life on earth is not real?

Tide: You mean like a dream?

Inspiration: Right! We live on earth only for a short period that is comparable to a dream. This dream was conceived when an idea of fear for food and desire for acquiring knowledge entered our consciousness. Remember the story of Adam and Eve. "*When the woman saw that the fruit of the tree was good for food and pleasing to the eye, and also desirable for gaining wisdom, she took some and ate it. She also gave some to her husband, who was with her, and he ate it"* (Gen. 3:6). We entered this deceptive reality when we were deceived to desire wisdom, depended on food for living and pleased our eyes with false images.

Bullet: This hypothesis does not concur even with the beliefs of organized religions. There is no evidence that our life on earth is a deception created by our own desires.

Inspiration: Yet, Jesus Christ proved that the desires of earthly life are deceptive. He taught people to not depend on earthly food but on every word of God. He taught people not to fear for earthly living but instead to worry about the death of the soul. He claimed to be the son of God who came from heaven. What is that heaven? Is it not a reality that we abandoned to live in the deception of earthly living by accepting the idea that we would die if we did not have earthly food? Has not Jesus preached an eternal life through resurrection from the death of this earthly life? Are not these hints that life on earth is only a deceptive dream created by our desires, and that resurrection to an eternal life is the reality that we missed when we succumbed to our desires?

Bullet: I originally started in the Church thinking the same. I wanted to live the spiritual life without worrying about the deceptions of the earthly life. However, the Church was heavily distracting me to worry about how people thought of me instead of my spiritual journey. I found that people do not like me and tried to earn their likability. Eventually I lost faith in the entire system of organized religions and abandoned my pursuit of the spiritual life. I believe that the sin that we, human beings, need salivation from is the desire to fit in the relations of earthly life. Life on earth is indeed a deception created by our own desires and wants.

Churchgoer: We go to the Church to be with God. You should not have allowed the politics to distract you.

Bullet: Right! I used to tell myself the same. However, the rituals in the Church are heavily influenced by its culture and even national politics. I once attended a church for the first time. Every one kept asking me "who are you?" I answered I am here to pray; I do not want to know your name and I do not want you to know my name. I just want to pray. But this did not go well with the Church. I sensed it and I stopped attending. You cannot attend a congregation without being forced to engage its politics. If you attend a church, you have to engage the people and their politics. There is not a church that would allow you to participate in spiritual practices without fully examining your religious and political views to ensure that you belong to the Church. Such a person is treated as an unwelcomed stranger who did not contribute to the funds of building the church, nor pays regular contributions to pay the church's expenses, nor is loyal to support the church's politics in the society. Eventually, if a person is not supportive of the church's politics they do not trust their spiritual practices either.

Tide: Do you want Churches to operate at loss. You want to attend the church for prayers but do not pay their cost.

Bullet: I am willing to pay an admission ticket to support their operating cost. I just do not want church politics to distract me from dedicating my energy to spiritual practices.

Tide: So you want to be anti-social in the church?

Bullet: No. I like to socialize and empathize with people. But I do not want the politics of any group of people to be forced on me.

Tide: What you want is already happening by televangelists; you can pay for a TV channel that provides you all the worship rituals that you want. You went even beyond the wishful thinking of organized religions to fantasize that our life on earth is a deceptive dream created by our desires. There is no evidence for any of these fantasies.

Bullet: You believe in science. You accepted quantum physics, which theorizes the existence of parallel universes. Can the spiritual life be a parallel dimension shielded from us by our desires? You accepted the theory of relativity that proposes a time dimension. You realized that ideas can be transported by electrons across the globe. Humanity has learned from the richness of communicating those ideas with remarkable speed using technology that connects people together. You accepted that our minds can comprehend realities that we could not have imagined a few centuries ago. Is it not possible that spiritual discoveries have not been proven because we have not reached yet an adequate capacity to discover them? Jesus Christ was an evidence that proved life on earth is a deceptive reality. Some people claim to prove the existence of this spiritual world by performing miracles that defies all natural forces.

Tide: Spiritual theories have not been empirically proven. There are indeed people who claimed or witnessed miracles but none of their claims can be reproduced when the experiment is repeated in a laboratory or under a controlled environment. These miraculous claims are nothing more than subjective experiences influenced by ideas that persuaded them of their wishful thinking as reality. Why would any rational being build their reality based on the subjective experiences of a few?

Bullet: It is not true. Spiritual theories can be proven. There are recognizable steps to be taken to successfully carry out spiritual experiments. Love is the first step.

Inspiration: Jesus Christ demonstrated that love is the first step towards resurrection (awakening from earthly death).

Bullet: Maybe you are right. I know that I missed the feeling of being loved, which caused me to drift aimlessly in this life. Love, even though it is not measurable in the same manner that an experiment in the lab could be measured, is still a remarkable step towards liberating people from their fears to reach peace with themselves and others. You cannot explain the power of love scientifically. The cycle of deceptions experienced on earth were caused by failures to love. Is that not a rational proof that love is a force that breaks through deceptions?

Tide: This discussion is outrageously irrational. You are both referring to life on earth as a deception. You fall back on an unprovable idea, God, and you fall back onto the Bible for support. Even though many of the biblical ideas have proven to be false. The biblical teachings that women are dependent on men and that they were created from men have been used by many societies to suppress women's rights.

Bullet: Wait a second! You cannot seriously blame this on God. Cultures that did not believe in the Bible did not treat women any better. Belief in God has enabled men to treat women with respect and dignity.

Tide: You, "Bullet," have already experienced life in organized religions but rejected it because you realized its deception. Those religions believe far more deeply than you do in the Bible. You disapprove of organized religions, but you cannot accept that God is a false idea implanted in the human psyche and that you are unable to break free from it. God is an idea, like a mind-virus, that takes hold of people to the extent that even if they cannot prove it they still try to rationalize it. It is wishful thinking.

Inspiration: The way I see it is that both of you are talking about the same thing. You, "Tide", express your disapproval of God as an idea that became a mind virus because of the mistakes made by the followers of organized religions; who used God as a concept to further their political interests in earthly life. "Bullet" too disapproves of organized religions because they turned God's image into an idol without practicing love, which is the spirit of God.

CRITICISM – BEWARE!

People often misunderstand the motivation for criticism. Leaders often act as if criticism is meant as a judgement on their conduct.

Criticism is first and foremost a means of self-expression. It is not a means of attacking others. A critical person is a loving, sensitive and intelligent person expressing their observations of their surroundings and examining the culture to present a researched analysis of the negative impact of the cultural failures on people. Criticism is a loving and selfless adventure.

Angry expressions of criticism is to be blamed on the cultural suppression of freedom of expression. A tolerant and liberal culture would promote, nurture and guide critical expressions because without them the culture would fail to identify its mistakes

Criticism can be beneficial because it helps the culture to avoid harm-causing behavior and thereby improve the quality of life for its members.

Even though Western European culture dominates the world today and was once the champion of the critique of reason and individual thought, you will likely be punished if you criticize social or governmental institutions. This is true regardless of the situation you may find yourself in, whether at work, in politics, or among your circle of friends. Even a popular idiom in the West is often used to chastise critical individuals: "You can catch more flies with honey than with vinegar."

A person who spends a great deal of their effort to study a topic concerning any social issue and produce a criticism is in fact a person who loved others to point out failures. Criticism gives people the opportunity to see themselves as others would see them and therefore give them the opportunity to learn and adjust. There is a lot of love in criticism. On the other hand, people who are hostile do not care to study issues and criticize events; instead they build prejudices and go to wars.

Why criticism has become such a bad word? The macro political environment is flawed and is pushing people towards patterns of death (addiction, violence, terrorism and suicide) and therefore criticism of individual actions does not bring any loving result. Criticism should be directed at the system instead of the individual actors in the system.

In the West, criticism and the freedom of expression were to be the means by which societies diffused disputes, preventing them from escalating into war. Freedom of expression is a useful tool in that it allows people the opportunity to express themselves concerning social events and to learn from their opponents. It can also alleviate feelings of resentment and dissension.

Unfortunately today criticism is rewarded only if exercised by rich nations toward poor nations or by affluent people toward less affluent people. It is a dishonest form of criticism. It is criticism by the power of authority, not by the power of reason. Westerners, in contrast to the rhetoric of their constitutions, are increasingly intolerant of criticism in public discourse. Rather, a new rhetoric of "positive thinking" has replaced the rhetoric of criticism.

The decline of public criticism, I suggest, has its roots in three recent shifts in society. These movements of the last three decades have increasingly impeded our ability to address the world's problems.

- The adherence to authority over respect for reason and the suppression of scientific criticism.

- The increasing corporatization of academia, leading academics to abandon their traditional role of critics of the system on behalf of the dispossessed and those who lack the education or means to present their grievances in society.

- Social pressures preventing third-world immigrants from expressing their criticism of their new societies.

Respect for Authority over Respect for Reason

Intelligent leaders welcome criticism because it sheds light on their hard work in representing the opposing views of the individual members of their constituency in a balanced manner. Inept leaders, on the other hand, fear criticism because it exposes their false pretenses in representing their constituents' needs. They threaten and punish dissenters. Many will go so far as to file libel suits against their own constituency.

Similarly, judges protect themselves from the public by issuing court sentences as a punishment for criticism.

In August of 2015, a Saskatoon man was punished for protesting a judge's ruling in family court ("Saskatoon man gets 17 months for harassing judge" [6]). The man placed posters containing assertions against the judge near the Family Law and Queen's Bench Court in Saskatoon. Despite the description of the man's actions as non-violent, the judge ruled the defendant guilty of harassment.

In May of 2016, a Las Vega judge was irritated by the attempt of a lawyer and deputy public defender to argue on behalf of her client despite his desire that she demonstrate respect for him by her silence and ordered her to be placed in handcuffs and seated next to inmates in court ("Judge Handcuffs Defense Attorney In Court To Teach Her 'A Lesson' For Speaking Out" [7]). This was a clear manifestation of the state of mind of the judiciary in our modern societies. They enforce their desire to be respected in their own manners over the rights of the individual to be represented.

Tragically, when average individuals read this kind of news, they fear punishment if they peacefully protest or criticize court decisions. Rather than function as instruments for dispute resolution, the courts enforce the power of authority, further deepening societal resentment. Such behavior demands absolute obedience to authority when dealing with the justice and law enforcement systems.

Current authorities appear to be less interested in debating whether you received a just treatment or not. Rather, they are to be obeyed.

People are likely to get better treatment if they silently obey authority rather than defend themselves and risk appearing disobedient. In our time, respect for authority supersedes reason.

The rise of absolute authority is also demonstrated in the shooting and death of a 19-year-old man by a police officer ("South Carolina officer shoots unarmed white teen during pot bust" [8]). The man, accused of driving a vehicle towards the officer, died of his injuries. Later examination of the evidence revealed the officers tampered with the evidence and abused their power to protect themselves. Such stories further lead people to believe that the police force is not protecting citizens but the state.

If this is the situation in the West, can you imagine how far more oppressive authorities appear in countries outside of the Western hemisphere, where people are routinely tortured in police stations for any infraction or for the slightest involvement in disputes? World authorities manufacture dissent and violence rather than resolve disputes because they seek to discontinue the means of criticism and representation for the average individual.

We have to ask ourselves, however: Who are the authorities? If an increasing number of citizens do not care to vote, who gets to occupy positions of authority?

Authorities are often placed in office by people disinterested in criticism or debates about justice. Authorities are increasingly interested in obedience and respect for their authority. Leaders are less interested in advancing the public good. Rather, they seek the "popular" vote and stage massive campaigns portraying an attractive image to their constituents.

Rather than take interest in the views and positions of their elected leaders, many in society have fallen prey to the cult of a leader and have succumbed to the idolization of their leaders. As long as their leader ensures their comfort and well-being, they have little regard for the person's concern for the justice of all in their community.

Elites Representing the Dispossessed

A society can damage people by excluding them from the benefits it offers to other members. The result is most visible in the world today where the gap between the rich and poor has widened. People who cannot take advantage of benefits such as employment opportunities and income within their own societies do not have the option of finding a living somewhere else because rich countries have closed their borders to them. They cannot emigrate to outer space.

The existence of societies has implicitly introduced the moral duty of a social contract towards every person in a given society. The social contract is an obligation for all elements of the society, and not only the government, to plan for the well-being of every member. Care for every member does not mean socialism and the central distribution of resources. It only means that whatever political structure and/or system of economy the society employs, whether capitalism or socialism, it must provide adequate opportunities for its members to live decently.

Throughout history it has been considered an honorable activity for the educated class of a society, called the intelligentsia, to criticize the political system on behalf of the dispossessed and the oppressed, who often cannot defend themselves. However, in recent years, many academics and scholars have been forced to search for better job conditions. The corporatization of academia—the decline of tenure-track positions and the casualization of academic labour (contracting out part-time, low-waged work that does not offer benefits)—makes it very difficult for academics to feel confident speaking out, for fear that their contracts will not be renewed. As a result, we see a decrease in the number of people willing to use peaceful measures to advocate for those divested of their rights, with an attendant rise in violent radicalism.

Osama Bin Laden was the world's most wanted terrorist when he was killed in 2011 by the U.S. Marines. Why did he earn an honorable position among many of his followers? He represented the dispossessed. Bin Laden was a university-educated Saudi billionaire who sacrificed his own comfort to represent the grievances of his people, whereas the Western-dominated media and the Western-backed military rulers of the Middle East have failed to represent their people. They have instead suppressed criticism and do not care to resolve the disputes of large segments of their populations.

The appeal of Bin Laden and other terrorist leaders has drawn people from distant places to join their campaigns. A news story in the *Calgary Herald* dated August 10, 2015, "Mother of Calgary man killed in Syria calls Harper terrorism plan 'window dressing'" [9], told of a young man from Calgary, Canada who converted to Islam at age 17 and died in Syria fighting with the Islamic State of Iraq and Syria (ISIS) at 22.

Why would a young man from a non-Muslim family join the ranks of terrorists who are fighting savage tribal wars? Syria is not his tribe. His family is Canadian. How could have he learned to become a religious fundamentalist of Islamic teachings and literature in only five years?

He likely was not a religious fundamentalist. He probably managed to learn only a few chapters of religious literature in those five years. Most of his five years in Islam was likely spent fighting for the cause of the oppressed, with little knowledge of the religious literature. The young man, like many other young people drawn to terrorist groups, was attracted to what he perceived as opposition to the oppression of free speech. If our society prohibits people from presenting their grievances and seeking resolutions to their disputes, then they can be easily deceived by organizations that fight against authorities. It happened that this person's conversion to Islam coincided with an era when terrorism is used as a front activity for defending the underdog. Therefore he probably went to fight because he wanted to "represent" more than he wanted to "practice" the teachings of his new religion.

It is the desire to represent the oppressed and marginalized—and not religious fundamentalism—that motivates people to join "terrorists." Think of the fictional movie character of Rambo (played by the famous actor Sylvester Stallone), an American who went to fight with Afghani jihadists against Soviet oppression. So-called terrorists of this ilk travel to oppressed regions to "represent" a population under siege below the watchful eyes of world authorities who fail to make peace in the area. Instead they supply the warring factions with weapons that kill innocent civilians.

The drive to "represent" the oppressed is an indication people are attempting to escape from the idolatry of leader worship that failed to represent their constituency. The level of freedom in society and the authority's responsiveness to the call for dispute resolution will determine which escape route they will take. If societies would successfully identify the damaging impact of idolatry, many youth would not fall into the trap of following terrorist organizations and would find avenues for their expressions of dissent. Western media air old stories of Robin Hood and various Hollywood movies, offering them as an alternative to the absence of representation. People in the West offer representations primarily on television or in movies—that is, in fiction, but not in reality. People are now addicted to fiction because they cannot meet their needs in reality. So great is their delusion that to find a reader like you, willing to spend hours reading a non-fiction book on idolatry instead of fiction, is a miracle.

Our ability to communicate has greatly diminished and has been replaced with the art of deception. Through honey-coated words and manufactured images on electronic devices, we are led to believe that if we remain complacent we will have a better chance at fortune, whereas if we criticize we will certainly create too many enemies and benefit no one. Criticism is suppressed under the pretense of promoting "positive thinking" and avoiding "negative thinking." Those of us living in urban areas have learned that "criticism is futile." There is no benefit to us for criticizing societal norms or standards. Rather, we prefer not to participate in any social activity in which we would find reason to criticize. Many of us will withdraw our children from the public education system because we do not agree with its values, and instead we form alternative education systems.

Not only the authorities, but urban dwellers in general, have learned to punish those among them who criticize—the way a critical academic such as Noam Chomsky, for example, was shunned by the U.S. mainstream media. Do you see the connection between chastising critical academics and youth seeking to represent the oppressed, albeit often misguided by their lack of research and insight into controversial topics? If society does not support academics, morally and financially, to engage in fierce debate, there will be unexplored issues, such as the topic of this book—idolatry—that academics will not cover.

If you search Amazon's website for a non-fiction book on idolatry, you will get only one title, published in 1998 by Moshe Halbertal, Avishai Margalit, and Naomi Goldblum. According to the book description, the book "examines the meaning and nature of idolatry— and, in doing so, reveals much about the monotheistic tradition that defines itself against this sin. The authors consider Christianity and Islam, but focus primarily on Judaism."

I asked myself: "Why is there not any secular research regarding such an important concept in human history?" Then I realized that what I wanted to express regarding idolatry was not written in a book and so I decided to write this book to start a public debate.

The consequences of the failure to vigorously criticize such controversial issues can be costly to society at large in terms of youth deceived into supporting texts and concepts that are beyond their skills to deconstruct and interpret.

Immigrants who arrive in the West with a critical mentality discover that they are singled out as "black sheep" if they express their critical opinions. Immigrants are expected to express only gratitude for and loyalty to a system that allowed them to belong to that elite club of one billion people who were chosen out of the seven billion of the earth's population. They had the privilege of making their way inside the heavily fortified borders of the Western hemisphere. Immigrants fear to criticize decisions made by authorities, lest they fall out of favor with their new societies and lose the privilege of citizenship in the West. The amount of fear that immigrants endure is not trivial.

In summary, the world is heading towards a situation where the richest one billion, the earth's elites, are actively defaming, instead of representing, the remaining six billion, in order to suppress their criticism. There is a gradual trend whereby the elites use the full force of technology to defame those who are marginalized, through accusations of terrorism to justify the abuse of power and authority. There are no winners in this situation. It is a lose-lose situation. Why? The elites so live under constant propaganda of their own making that they are terrified of the marginalized, whereas the marginalized live under constant propaganda that says they are oppressed. As you finish reading this book you will realize the destructive impact of idolatry on the human race.

The Failure to Tolerate Criticism

Criticism has a role in building a representative leadership and an intellectual community that can exercise checks and balances on the excesses of the leadership. The suppression of individual freedom to criticize a group's activity leads to a culture of idolatry where higher value is placed on the other's perception of opinion of the person. A culture of this sort focuses on collecting admirers and avoiding any adversaries in order to capture the rewards of pooling the favors and goodwill of many people towards the individual.

The idolatry of the human race has produced a modern class of leadership that, in essence, is the priests and priestesses of Baal. They desire, even worship, social acceptance, fame, and money while keeping a population of seven billion forever deceived with a rhetoric of insufficient resources for living. Yet, scientific evidence contradicts that claim.

Let me draw on another example of a culture that suppressed criticism to the extent that people turned to idolatry. In the 1990s the Serbs were driven to total ignorance out of their desire to win the war against neighboring Bosnia. They reached a state of denial when the world classified their actions as genocide against Bosnia. If the culture had adequate internal forces of self-criticism, it might not have become that blinded by desire to win the war.

IDOLATRY VS. REASON

The desires of the flesh that lead to sexual immorality, the desire for military power that leads to murder, the desire to acquire authority over people that creates rulers instead of representatives of people, and the lust for appropriating wealth (beyond one's daily needs) to acquire sex, power and authority over people are all forms of idolatry.

Worshiping the monotheistic God under group pressure is a form of idolatry in which the person is deceived by a false image of God imposed by the group pressure that often does not lead to peace and love as observed in the fighting between the followers of major organized religions.

Idols traditionally meant images or forms that the individual holds sacred. The Judeo-Christian scriptures describe idolatry as the worship of images or forms: "You shall not make for yourself an image in the form of anything in heaven above or on the earth beneath or in the waters below. You shall not bow down to them or worship them" (Exodus 20:4-5).

The secular meaning, on the other hand, identifies idolatry as the excessive or blind adoration of any person, thing, or activity. It can also be understood as the desire to find an idol that gives a sense of self-worth or a sense of safety from adversity in life on earth.

Looking for someone's approval to provide a sense of self-worthiness instead of generating it internally is termed the "Cinderella Syndrome" in modern literature but I argue that it should be redefined as "idolatry."

The interpretation and identification of sensory information can be a source of misperception; for example, ancient civilizations used to worship the sun because of the interpretation of its energy as a source of life.

The story of our human societies begins with Adam and Eve. Therefore this is the point out of which we should start our examination of idolatry and its impact on our societies.

Adam and Eve were created innocent and pure and dwelled in a garden. In the middle of the garden stood a tree with the deceptive image of an eye-pleasing fruit. However, Adam and Eve were warned by their Creator that "the day that you eat from it you will surely die" (Genesis 2:17).

"What kind of death awaits a person from eating a fruit?", people question. Eating from that fruit did not cause a cessation of blood circulation and breathing in the bodies of Adam and Eve according to the Biblical story. The incident marked a different meaning of death than the bodily kind.

The incident was humanity's first experience of desire based on the perception of deceptive images of pleasure. The forbidden tree was the first idol experienced by humankind. Adam and Eve disobeyed a warning from their Creator to avoid surrendering to the desire posed by that fruit. Idolatry involves willfully turning away from reason towards objects of inferior morality.

Therefore to understand the meaning of idolatry we have to consider the meaning of its opposite, namely reason. If we identify the principle of reason upon which humanity was created it will be easier to identify the principles of its opposite, namely idolatry.

Characteristics of Reason

> *"In the beginning was the Word, and the Word was with God,*
> *and the Word was God" (John 1:1).*

In the following sections I enumerate what I call the characteristics of reason that are directly related to the subject of idolatry. This is not meant as an exhaustive list of the Biblical references to reason (that the Creator communicated to humankind), which would include the Ten Commandments; rather it is a selective list meant to serve as the basis for an explanation of the meaning of idolatry. I devised this list when my family challenged me to explain what is considered reason in contrast to idolatry. What are the characteristics of a reason-filled life?

#1 Be Fruitful

Chronologically, the first communication regarding reason that humans comprehended concerning their existence was, "Be fruitful and increase in number; fill the earth and subdue it. Rule over the fish in the sea and the birds in the sky and over every living creature that moves on the ground" (Gen. 1:28). These were the first words of reason regarding existence that humanity received after creation.

Humankind was created to be fruitful, to fill the earth, to rule over the creatures inhabiting it. We were shaped in the likeness of God. Humans are the only species capable of expressing reason through language: "When God created humankind, he made them in the likeness of God. He created them male and female and blessed them. And he named them 'humankind' when they were created" (Gen. 5:1-2).

God, the ultimate source of reason, commanded humankind to fill the earth and to rule over its creatures. In our modern era, some modern scientists reason that the earth is overpopulated and cannot provide adequate resources for the lives of its seven billion inhabitants, which is still a population that has not filled the massive empty lands of the earth. One ought to question their reasoning, particularly when there is plenty of scientific reasoning that the earth is not overpopulated.

Humanity continuously struggles to discern truth from deception by the power of reason. As you finish reading this book, you will understand my argument that idolatry is the cause of the problem of abandoning reason and instead following impressive figures of authority.

#2 Man shall not live on bread alone

The story of creation provides the first lesson on the consequences of idolatry. Adam and Eve faced a situation in which they had to choose between reason and the allure of a deceptive image. God created a garden containing every tree that is pleasing to the eye and good for food: "The Lord God made all kinds of trees grow out of the ground— trees that were pleasing to the eye and good for food" (Gen. 2:9).

In the midst of this garden God placed a lesson to humanity about the dangers of abandoning reason. He planted a tree that brings death, and warned Adam of its deadly effect: "you must not eat from the tree of the knowledge of good and evil, for when you eat from it you will certainly die" (Gen. 2:17).

Imagine if you were to go to the pharmacy and pick up medicine that the pharmacist labeled as toxic if ingested. If you were to ignore the warning label because you liked the appearance of the medicine and ingested it, would you have acted on reason or passion?

Similarly, Adam and Eve fell into idolatry, surrendering their will to the temptation of an image of an eye-pleasing fruit even though they were given reason to believe it was deadly: "When the woman saw that the fruit of the tree was good for food and pleasing to the eye, and also desirable for gaining wisdom, she took some and ate it. She also gave some to her husband, who was with her, and he ate it" (Gen. 3:6).

The so-called "original sin", upon which many religious doctrines have been built, is the idolatry of surrendering one's will (obedience) to the temptations of images, contrary to reason. There was a temptation to gain wisdom—against solid reason to believe in the certain death that this fruit would bring. Adam and Eve gambled to gain wisdom and neglected their capacity to reason.

> *The tempter came to him and said, "If you are the Son of God, tell these stones to become bread."*
>
> *Jesus answered, "It is written: 'Man shall not live on bread alone, but on every word that comes from the mouth of God.'"*
>
> *Matthew 4:3-4*

The salvation delivered by Christ from original sin is the triumph over idolatry in its various forms, among which are the temptation of wealth, the temptation of an earthly kingdom, and the temptation to avenge one's injured dignity.

The children of Adam and Eve did not comprehend the lesson of Creation. They did not understand the danger of abandoning reason to obey desire. It turned out that humans would need to undertake a long journey to learn the power of reason and to reject idolatry in order to understand the difference between life and death—a journey we are still on.

What does it mean to be alive and what does it mean to be dead? The answer lies in the power of reason and the rejection of idolatry. Reason leads to eternal spiritual life but idolatry leads to a deceptive temporal life and spiritual death.

#3 Whoever Wants to Become Great Among You Must Be Your Servant

> *"Jesus called them together and said, 'You know that those who are regarded as rulers of the Gentiles lord it over them, and their high officials exercise authority over them. Not so with you. Instead, whoever wants to become great among you must be your servant, and whoever wants to be first must be slave of all. For even the Son of Man did not come to be served, but to serve, and to give his life as a ransom for many.'" Mark 10:42-45*

The Biblical measure explained in Mark 10:42-45 is the most accurate method for identifying cultures that worship idols. If the culture is managed by authoritarian rulers then it is an idol-worshipping culture. If the culture is democratic, such that those who lead are the servants of the society, then it is not an idol-worshipping culture.

#4 Thou Shalt Not Kill

Tragically, we learn later in the story of Genesis about the murder of Abel by his brother Cain. It is another lesson to humanity about the impact of deceptive images on human behavior controlled by desire instead of reason.

The perception of respect, which Cain desired but did not receive, created a deceptive sense of injury to Cain's dignity that caused him to kill his brother Abel. Although some regard the story as myth, it reminds us that people murder each other over their perception of injury to their dignity—dignity that they desire but do not receive.

What happens when someone feels disadvantaged as the other in any given situation? Will they accept reason or will desire push them to avenge their sense of injured dignity?

This is the second lesson to humanity about idolatry: obedience to images is motivated by desire instead of reason.

God's favoring of Abel's offering exposed Cain's false image of the respect he expected from God by virtue of being the older brother. Favoring one person's gift over another's should not be more than a trivial incident in any family: "The Lord looked with favor on Abel and his offering, but on Cain and his offering he did not look with favor. So Cain was very angry, and his face was downcast" (Gen. 4:4-5).

However, Cain's action represented not a single incident but rather a behavioral pattern that motivates wars between human beings who avenge their injured dignity. God attempted to guide Cain toward reason instead of desire to rule over false images of dignity: "But if you do not do what is right, sin is crouching at your door; it desires to have you, but you must rule over it" (Gen 4:7).

#5 Do not be afraid of those who kill the body but cannot kill the soul

The world's religious literature about Jesus Christ offers a contrary lesson, an example of triumph over the deceptive image of injury to one's dignity. Christ, charged with blasphemy and subversion of the worldly authority, was humiliated and crucified as a terrorist. Rather than avenge the injustice done to him, Christ provides a model of triumph over desire by adhering to what is true and good. It is a triumph over idolatry.

Fear of other people is the result of idolatry that created a population of people abusing each other.

Many people appreciate the solitude of life in the wilderness because humans have become so abusive to one another. Abuse is the result of idolatry; that is, the result of following deceptive images that turn people away from God to inferior objects of moral values that turn them into murderers and abusers.

The individual's fear of God's creatures and loss of trust in God's wisdom and power is a form of idolatry. God created every soul for a reason. Excessive fear of other people is the underlying motive for racism where fear of the increased population of any demographic group becomes a reason to harm them.

The desire to belong to social networks, whereby the individual degrades those who do not belong to the same social networks, is an idol that causes the individual to devalue God's creation. People worship the social structures that materially benefit them and condemn those who refuse to follow their social rules.

In certain social structures the individual is expected to follow the timing and the manners of what to believe based on the leader's desires; that is, it is not a matter of what to believe in but rather when to believe in it based on obedience to the governing power. You can be made to believe in one thing at certain times and in its opposite at other times if your belief complies with conformity to authority. In such cases, obedience is falsely claimed propagandized as a virtue and criticism is not welcome; therefore it becomes the perfect culture for idolatry. Any social structure that demands your obedience but becomes hostile to your criticism is a culture of idolatry. It becomes xenophobic towards those who do not belong to its social circles.

Idolatry Redefined

Now that I have discussed the principles of Biblical reason, let me refine my concept of idolatry, which, as I said, is the opposite of reason.

An idol is any false idea or image (material or conceptual) that appears pleasurable but in fact when followed carries death and runs contrary to the principles of reason that humanity was created to fulfill.

Any claim to suppress human reproduction for fear of material want is an idol (a false image of reason that carries death).

Any claim to fear for lack of daily bread that forces people to fight and kill is an idol. Any claim to leadership based on the desire for fame and power is an idol. Any claim to kill in the name of God is an idol. Any claim to fear the demographic growth of foreigners or any ethnic group is an idol. Any claim for security that requires suppression of criticism is an idol.

To expand on this argument, I suggest that any image shielded from criticism, whether material or ideological, is an idol. Any image or idea open to criticism is not an idol. If you find yourself in an activity that forbids criticism, then you have landed in a culture of idolatry that suppresses your reasoning ability and diminishes your intellect.

I propose the tolerance of criticism as a litmus test for identifying idolatry.

Idolatry, therefore, can only be understood within the subjective context of the person and not in absolute terms of existing images that are conceived in the mind or painted or sculpted by people.

One can own a painting or a statue that one does not shield from criticism and therefore is not a source of idolatry. Paintings, works of art, and sculptures are not idols until someone decides to protect them from criticism, at which time the image becomes an idol. An idea or desire that one obsesses over and guards against criticism is an idol.

A person who tolerates criticism of an idea or object acknowledges that the idea or object is inherently flawed. If one's sense of dignity is above criticism, it becomes an idol and can lead one to become obsessed with one's own image. Such a person will enforce others' respect of their person most often by means of violence, as described in the story of Cain's murder of Abel, and as in the case of most wars between nations of the world.

Consider the situation of cults that enforce deference to their system and stifle any opposition among their members. Such cults are idolatrous in the sense that they value "respect" toward the authority of their social structure more than they value the scientific process of inquiry and the need for continuous change to improve, which requires criticism.

A follower of a religion who shields religious doctrine from criticism worships an idol. This form of idolatry has caused brutal religious wars in human history. Many of these wars were caused by believers' insistence that they were the only chosen people who would enter paradise and that those who did not adhere to the same religious doctrine would be thrown into hell.

I invite you to consider both the secular and the religious meanings of idolatry, whether you are an atheist or a believer in God. In doing so, I seek to liberate the concept of idolatry from the constraints of religious doctrine. The freedom to believe or doubt the presence of God is an entirely different subject. One can doubt the presence of God (be an atheist) and still avoid the negative behavioral impacts of idolatry if one accepts criticism and practices self-criticism. I stress this point, as the goal of my book is not to invite you, the reader, to believe in God or any religion. My goal is to highlight the negative consequences of holding idols, whether in cognitive or material forms, above criticism.

Let me illustrate my understanding of idolatry in a religious context. Assume that a person who believes in jihad (fighting in the name of God) argues that God's commandments are above criticism because God is the only perfect spirit in the universe. Since God commanded jihad (according to the religious literature in which the jihadi believes) one has to obey the instructions for jihad without criticizing them. The difficulty in this point is that the conclusion that God commanded jihad is only an image formed by one's perception because God has not appeared to that person (as the person proposing the counter-argument would readily agree). Therefore the notion that God commanded jihad was constructed based on one's trust in the religious literature available in one's culture. Therefore the person committed idolatry even though they thought they were ardent enemies of idolatry because they held the interpretation of the religious text above criticism in the absence of any real encounter with the spirit of God.

If one subjects all ideas or objects to criticism, then one becomes free from the negative impact of idolatry. If one believes in worshipping God and avoids all icons and images but holds above criticism the religious interpretation of text, as the Church stood against the criticism of the scientific revolution during the Middle Ages, then one equally suffers the negative impact of idolatry. It is in tolerating criticism that one liberates oneself from idolatry.

The problem with religion is the perception that it tries to persuade people to follow and obey, without criticism, religious leadership or elders; in turn, this blind obedience becomes an idolatry in which criticism is not allowed. If a religious dress code, or a rule on women's behavior, becomes a topic beyond criticism then it becomes an idol that one worships.

If a place of worship becomes more sacred than human life to a group of people then they engage in idolatry. Jesus Christ is reported to have expressed this concept in the Biblical passage, "Destroy this temple, and I will raise it again in three days" (John 2:19). The stone-made temple was sacred to the people who lived around the time of Jesus to the extent that it warranted people sacrificing their lives to protect it. Jesus instead demonstrated that the goal is eternal life (resurrection) and not the stone-made temple. In many places in the world today, followers of monotheistic religions are fighting and offering their lives to protect stone-made places of worship under the conviction that the place carries a sacred blessing to them. It is idolatry in which stone-carved figures have assumed more value than human lives.

In essence many followers of monotheistic religions can become more idolatrous than those who doubt the presence of God. Conversely those who doubt the presence of God can be more faithful to the practice of the first commandment than those who profess to believe in the God of the Ten Commandments.

An example is a recent murder case reported on CBS titled "Suspect in deadly on-air attack blamed Charleston shooting" [10] in which a former employee at CBS claimed, in a written memo, that Jehovah spoke to him and told him to act. "The writer said he suffered racial discrimination, sexual harassment, and bullying at work—stemming from him being a gay, black man, ABC News reports." He murdered two other CBS employees before killing himself as a result of his belief. It is a case of severe idolatry even though the person claimed to believe in God. The person's perception of being a victim of racial discrimination and sexual harassment became so idolatrous that it overcame his ability to reason. This is clear evidence that a claim to belief in God is not necessarily a guarantee against idolatry.

> *"Not everyone who says to me, 'Lord, Lord,' will enter the kingdom of heaven, but only the one who does the will of my Father who is in heaven. Many will say to me on that day, 'Lord, Lord, did we not prophesy in your name and in your name drive out demons and in your name perform many miracles?' Then I will tell them plainly, 'I never knew you. Away from me, you evildoers!'"*

Matthew 7:21-23

The fear that drives one person to kill another is a form of idolatry. The fear that a leader arouses in a follower to convince the follower to go to war to kill is a form of idolatry that involves a deceptive image—the leader deceives the follower to shield the leader's decision from criticism.

A news article in the Washington Post on October 2, 2015, titled "Slain victims of mass shooting at Oregon college identified" [11], told about a shooting incident in a college in Oregon. A student purportedly questioned his fellow students at gunpoint about their religious affiliation. He killed those who answered that they belonged to an organized religion and spared those who answered otherwise. As one witness described it, the shooter would ask "Are you Christian?," then say, "'Good, because you're a Christian, you're going to see God in just about one second,' and then he shot and killed them." In a second article related to the murder another student explained that the shooter did not single out Christians, instead he just sarcastically consoled his victims with the claim that they would go to heaven after he killed them. This is an example of an idea that became an idol that overwhelmed a person's capacity for reasoning and consequently led to death.

God is the source of reason. Any reasoning that leads to murder is an idol—a false reasoning that leads to death. God commanded that "thou shalt not kill." A person who follows an idea in violation of God's commandments is worshipping an idol.

Our world is full of deceptions that are the forces of idolatry regardless of one's belief or doubt in the existence of God.

Forces that change one's conscience by painting cognitive images of social rewards become an idolatry of those images and rewards, and of those holding the power of authority over others.

Consider a person who seeks a leadership position because of the desire for fame and power, not because he is capable of resolving disputes, and representing and planning for his constituency. Such a person becomes addicted to the image of being in authority but gives little honest service to his constituency. This is the kind of leadership that we see in the world today: leaders who enforce their authority by threats of violence toward their people.

I had a recent experience with the top executive of a volunteer organization of which I was a member for six months. I expressed a criticism of the elections in the organization. I called the elections non-representative. My criticism of the elections confronted his authority over his established network of some 2000 members who abided by his every word. He removed my access to the group's Facebook page so that my criticisms were not published. He further threatened to ban me from the organization until I resigned from the group. This event was trivial in its social impact on me because it only involved a volunteer organization. However, it motivated me to write this book to expand on the difference between leadership and the idolatry of worshiping the power of authority. If having authority in a social network of only a couple thousand members can be that intoxicating, then how much more intoxicating is the effect of being in authority over an entire nation?

Idolatry impacts an individual's mentality and psychology. Idolatry diminishes a person's intellectual capacity because the individual's perceptions become shackled by false images. Idolatry distorts a person's conscience to accept deceptions and become hostile to those who criticize those deceptions.

The change in the person's valuations of "right and wrong" impacts their psychology. The concept of "respect" for idolaters becomes a function of pleasing their desires, rather than a function of achieving fairness, justice or prosperity for every member of the population.

Idolatry promotes selfishness: "Why should I care for my brother?" In contrast, conscientious people find a great deal of happiness in achieving solutions that meet the needs of every person in the population.

Had the earth's population observed the lessons learned about the negative consequences of idolatry from our ancestors (the story of Adam and Eve and of Cain and Abel), we would have used our intellect and reason to plan for all seven billion of the earth's population, and we would have resolved the disputes among populations using dispute resolution mechanisms.

I do not merely use the term idolatry. I argue that idolatry is the true cause of societal failure and offer an alternative understanding of the term. I am deconstructing our understanding of idolatry.

The relationship between idolatry and the failure of societies is real and is not something that I imagine to exist.

A cursory review of the recent destruction of historical artifacts by terrorist groups such as the Taliban and ISIS illustrates the powerful connection between idolatry and terrorism. As early as March 2001, Taliban leader Mullah Mohammed Omar ordered the destruction of the Buddhas of Bamiyan, two sixth-century monumental statues of the Buddha carved into the side of a cliff in the Bamiyan Valley in

Afghanistan. Omar declared the statues to be idolatrous. Later envoys from the United States suggested that the images were also destroyed out of regional anger toward the Afghan government's financial maintenance of the statues despite famine.

For nearly fourteen centuries these historic artifacts existed without any accusation of idolatry. They were nothing more than tourist attractions. Why then, in recent decades, have terrorist organizations expressed their frustration through destruction of these historic sites, whereas all Islamic civilizations of the past fourteen centuries were not bothered by their presence?

Terrorist groups perceive the images as representative of the idolism of national leaders. In their attempt to undermine the authorities, the terrorists direct their anger toward symbolic items as way of bringing media attention more than any relief of their grievances. It is for this reason that I explore idolatry in this book and examine its underlying role in the problems of leadership and authority that contribute to terrorism.

I will address the importance of criticizing authorities' mistakes that caused the problem of terrorism. I will also assert the importance of a peaceful solution whose goal is to please God, not people.

I will address the problem of obedience in all of this. When is obedience a virtue and when is it idolatry?

In our contemporary world, everyone and every nation brought upon themselves the trials they face in following the desire for deceptive images, or idols.

Everyone is guilty despite the fact that everyone employs various methods to prove their innocence in the sight of others.

God is just and is in control of the world despite the media propaganda and the mistaken beliefs to the contrary.

> *The Lord is in his holy temple; the Lord is on his heavenly throne.*
> *He observes everyone on earth; his eyes examine them.*

The Lord examines the righteous, but the wicked, those who love violence, he hates with a passion.

Psalm 11: 4-5

To prove that it is more important to please God by adhering to peace in the face of adversity, rather than trying to prove the guilt of others by force, let me take the example of the Biblical story of Joseph.

Joseph is an example of reacting to injustice by peaceful means while focusing on pleasing God rather than pleasing people. Joseph's brothers attempted to malign Joseph in the sight of his father to win their father's favor. They attempted to kill Joseph, but he lived because of God's will. They attempted to malign their brother in the sight of his father, but he was exalted and honored by God's will. They sold Joseph as a slave, yet by God's will he was elevated to become a powerful king. The story of Joseph is a perfect example of how the desire of men to prove themselves to others can lead to violence and how those who seek God's will by reacting peacefully towards hostility will be favored and elevated by God's will.

I will explain all these concepts in light of my understanding of the Biblical first commandment.

It is my belief that the first commandment of the Bible was established to foster and encourage healthy human behavior. The first of the Ten Commandments was the single greatest triumph of reason over idolatry. Humankind's faith in the first commandment is the most solid foundation of reason for human societies.

Our societies are full of expressions of wisdom uttered by philosophers, leaders and even celebrities. Few of them are helpful. They can only distract and deceive. Only one voice is helpful and guiding. It is the voice of Reason and Love. God is Love and also the Word of Reason.

Images in the media of leaders meeting in extravagant palaces making pronouncements about world affairs are not helpful; they are misleading. The proof of this claim is the current situation of violence and social inequality, which is a symptom of a misled humanity.

Followers that exert their efforts to win votes for one leader or one party are not helpful; they are misleading. People who put their hope for change in leaders also damage their own credibility when those same leaders act based on the desire to keep their position of fame rather than do what is right.

There is only one force of guidance in the universe. This force is God. God is not a delusion. Although people's perceptions of God can be delusional to satisfy their desires, God remains constant.

People create gods out of idols (deceptive images) that please their desires. However, God is a constant force of Reason and Love that lacks deception.

Where to find the word of God? In the voice of one's conscience and in independently examining the Bible.

One might argue that this is an exaggeratedly grim perspective. Not all people in urban cities are pedophiles or slave masters. There are doctors, engineers and highly educated elites. What good is it to have highly educated elites working for and contributing to political forces on global levels that profiteer from the weapons, drug and sex trades?

Understanding that idolatry causes this dysfunction of slavery in societies puts the moral responsibility for a solution on both the supplier and the consumer. Why would a poor person accept slavery? Wouldn't it be better to peacefully die with the moral conviction to worship God alone instead of serving other masters? Why would there be customers to acquire slaves in the world if they had the conviction to truly worship God alone? (The topic of what defines true worship is discussed in another chapter in this book.)

People in countries plagued with political and social dysfunction are often provoked by the elites' interest in historic monuments and art works to the extent that these artifacts are traded for millions of dollars whereas the individual human being is sold as slave labor for a few hundred dollars. Historic monuments and works of arts in this context have become idols that assume higher value than human lives. What is the impact of this idolatry? Severe social dysfunction. Imagine the confusion that results from valuing Islamic historic architecture worth millions of dollars when the Islamists who advocate a return to the Islamic civilization that produced this architecture are thrown in prisons, tortured and killed! This difference in the valuation of works of art versus human lives contributes to the terrorists desire to demolish such works.

I am not complaining. I believe that every trial is allowed for a good reason—so that we understand the consequences of worshipping idols and our failure to trust in God. Our societies are failing because people who experience such negative interactions understand that the rhetoric of democracy, liberty and freedom is only deceptive propaganda, and hiding behind it is a tremendous amount of slavery and social dysfunction.

The world around us is violent but one's inner world does not have to be. Peaceful thoughts and trust in God are the keys to quality of life despite the surrounding social reality. If one's thoughts turn violent, then one went down the wrong road because God is a god of peace and those who are filled with the spirit of God are peaceful. If the followers of an organized religion kill their opponents then their religion is not from God.

The Lord is in his holy temple; the Lord is on his heavenly throne.
He observes everyone on earth; his eyes examine them.

The Lord examines the righteous, but the wicked, those who love
violence, he hates with a passion.

Psalm 11: 4-5

TERRORISM

Idolatry caused terrorism because deceptions cause people to revolt. What kind of revolution should a person participate in—a peaceful revolution of the mind or a political revolution that requires armed force?

Before I go further into the topic of terrorism, let me clarify that I am not presenting an apologia for terrorism. I am presenting an analysis of its causes and a strategy for finding inner peace in a world of rampant violence.

I believe that the world is just even with people committing violations against one another because I believe that God is in control of the world. Every trial is allowed for a good reason. God allows every individual trial for good reason: to promote trust in God in the midst of adversity, and to improve the individual's chances of finding the way to eternal life. Therefore there is not injustice under the leadership of God in this universe even though people misbehave towards one another. Our role is to understand the causes of problems, to trust in God, and to triumph peacefully over adversity.

The problem is not the presence of terrorists; rather it is the presence of deceptive social systems that incite terrorists to prove that the authorities are unjust. Exposing the deceptive nature of the authorities would render unnecessary the need of people to prove the obvious by force. This is why I stress the importance of criticism in this book.

The importance of criticizing the mistakes of those who control the economic and social systems lies in guarding against the continuously confusing and misleading impact on the ordinary person, who is able to sense that something is wrong but unable to rationalize it, and who consequently falls into the trap of reacting violently.

If the population remains silent regarding the mistakes of the ruling economic and social elites, and continues to condemn only the "terrorists," then people will lose sight of the cause of the problem, which eventually impacts their children as victims of violence, poverty, the drug trade, the weapons industry, and sexual assault. All these problems are manifest in most modern societies.

The number of victims of social inequality, drugs, alcohol, sex, and weapons abuse are several times higher than the number of victims of acts of political terror. The number of victims of human trafficking alone every year exceeds the number of victims of political terrorism.

> *Trafficking in persons is a serious crime and a grave violation of human rights. Every year, thousands of men, women and children fall into the hands of traffickers, in their own countries and abroad. Almost every country in the world is affected by trafficking, whether as a country of origin, transit or destination for victims.*
>
> *Quoted from the "United Nations Office on Drugs and Crime" UNODC website*
>
> *https://www.unodc.org/unodc/en/human-trafficking/what-is-human-trafficking.html*

Who are the customers of human trafficking?

They are wealthy elites that can afford the heavy cost of the sexual exploitation of their victims merely to satisfy their worship of the idol of sexual assault (as opposed to normal sexual desires that can be legitimately fulfilled through marriage).

A person can be married with minimal financial cost if they find reciprocated feelings of love and care toward another person, whereas those who enjoy sexual exploitation must spend hundreds of thousands of dollars on acquiring sex slaves. One cannot acquire sex slaves for free.

The wealthy elites of our societies (that are plagued with idolatry) should be considered a far greater potential security risk than political terrorists. If there were not any wealthy customers for sexually exploited people, the business of human trafficking would collapse and cease to exist. Why then are there wealthy people willing to spend fortunes on sexual exploitation? The cause is idolatry.

Idolatry leads to an abusive lifestyle that manifests itself in various forms of moral and physical assault. Have you noticed that the security apparatuses of oppressive governments assault people's freedom by unlawfully kidnapping and detaining them, torturing them to death, or assaulting them sexually? Idolatry is an abusive lifestyle that starts with obeying deceptive images (of power, money or sex) that appear pleasurable but bring death.

Yet the authorities and the media distract their audiences from the violence caused by idolatry, claiming that the "War on Terror" is the single most important focus of our social system that deserves massive spending in terms of tax dollars directed toward military buildup and a willingness on the part of the populace to go to war against the terrorists.

The recent events of the terrorist attacks in Belgium (in March 2016) and France (in November 2015) ignited a debate about the failure of integrating European-born individuals into the culture of Europe. It also brought to light the impact of societal anger on home-grown terrorism.

The satisfaction of life among first- and second- generation migrants to the West depends on their sense of being loved or socially accepted. Migrants who have high social cohesion in their native cultures fare better than those who come from abusive cultures or from war-torn societies. Multiculturalism in the West has enabled every culture to have its own specific conditions compared to other subcultures within the country.

Those who do not belong to any culture in the West feel isolated and eventually live in abusive conditions that breed frustration. The culture of every community gives a major boost to its members' sense of confidence and acceptance within the multicultural society.

Therefore I make the assumption that Western-born terrorists are individuals whose immediate culture failed to provide a sense of respect and acceptance. But it is not the only factor contributing to their radicalization. Another factor is the loss of trust in the moral foundation of a Western world that allows social inequality to devour its own children through drug addiction, alcoholism, the sex trade and violence, in blatant contrast to its political rhetoric about human rights and equality.

The most important factor that determines the success of any person confronting such deceptions is the individual sense of responsibility, which protects one's integrity even in the midst of adversity.

A sense of acceptance by society is the first line of defense against terrorism but it is not the solution because human societies have always been plagued with deceptions (idols) that have carried various forms of (spiritual) death. Therefore it becomes important to build a sense of individual responsibly to deal with the loss of trust in a society whose rhetoric of human rights is not matched by its social reality. If the individuals comprising any given society develop a strong moral sense of individual responsibility then eventually the society, as a collection of individuals, will improve its reality to match its rhetoric. The individual is the nuclear unit of the society and therefore if every individual took the initiative to become morally responsible (instead of waiting for others to turn around first) then eventually the society would grow morally stronger.

Criticism is essential to identifying social failures; but changing other people by criticism alone will not bring the desired results. If the solution that one desires does not exist then one has to start by changing one's own behavior and values in order to change the immediate world with God's help.

A high level of democracy within society deters terrorism. People who are born in oppressed societies and live under abusive authoritarian conditions continue to wither under the curse of feeling unloved or unaccepted even after they immigrate to the West, where they continue to circle for generations around their origin's cultural paradoxes, attempting to find a solution.

The military support of Western governments for dictatorships in various parts of the world exacerbates those migrants' sense of alienation within the political cultures of the West.

Individuals who are tempted to follow violent means to deal with their sense of cultural dissatisfaction lose their ability to assume full responsibility for their own actions and become agents of the dysfunction within their cultures.

The cure is to strengthen the individual's sense of responsibility and capacity to triumph by peaceful means over the trials of life. This is the spirit of the Biblical teachings. Life on earth is a short journey (of less than 120 years) during which the individual's main responsibility is to triumph over evil thoughts brought on by the dysfunction of human society.

The goal of life is not achieving justice on earth by any means. The real goal is eternal life. It is triumphing over evil by God's peace. Without trials on earth, the individual would not have the opportunity to prove his or her triumph over violence by God's peace in exactly the same model presented by Jesus Christ. The role of every person is to find a peaceful resolution to the deceptions that they face in their trials on earth.

> *For our struggle is not against flesh and blood, but against the rulers, against the authorities, against the powers of this dark world and against the spiritual forces of evil in the heavenly realms. Therefore put on the full armor of God, so that when the day of evil comes, you may be able to stand your ground, and after you have done everything, to stand. Stand firm then, with the belt of truth buckled around your waist, with the breastplate of righteousness in place, and with your feet fitted with the readiness that comes from the gospel of peace. In addition to all this, take up the shield of faith, with which you can extinguish all the flaming arrows of the evil one. Take the helmet of salvation and the sword of the Spirit, which is the word of God.*
>
> *And pray in the Spirit on all occasions with all kinds of prayers and requests. With this in mind, be alert and always keep on praying for all the Lord's people.*
>
> *Ephesians 6: 12-18*

Attempting to prove things to people, as opposed to seeking one's desires through God, can lead to violence. The attempts of terrorists to prove that the rulers are deceptive are directed at winning support from people instead of from God. Both the rulers and the terrorists attempt to play on the fears of one segment of the population or another. The authorities play on the populace's fear of fatal attacks by terrorists, and the terrorists play on the impoverished populace's fear of the continued degradation of their living conditions under their ruler's authority. Both fears are false because God is in firm control of the world. There is not a trial that befell any person that escaped the sight of God.

> *Do not be afraid of those who kill the body but cannot kill the soul. Rather, be afraid of the One who can destroy both soul and body in hell. Are not two sparrows sold for a penny? Yet not one of them will fall to the ground outside your Father's care. And even the very hairs of your head are all numbered. So don't be afraid; you are worth more than many sparrows.*

> *Matthew 10: 28-31*

I differentiate between analyzing the situation as the product of the rise of corrupt rulers over world affairs and as the desire to stage armed campaigns to bring down the authority of those rulers, in accordance with Jesus Christ's instructions to:

- lay down one's sword,

- trust in God's will instead of seeking to prove the guilt of others to the people,

- not fear those who can kill the body,

- seek the kingdom of heaven which is only reserved for those who seek peace, and

- give to Caesar what's Caesar's and give to God what is God's.

I acknowledge that the world's nations are ruled by morally defective individuals who alienated and exercised unprecedented armed violence over their respective populations to steal their wealth.

There is a difference between the rulers and the elected politicians.

Financial interests rule over politicians and over the people's will by controlling the media. Elected politicians have been reduced to opportunists seeking better paying jobs and better retirement benefits.

I also acknowledge that their opponents (the so-called terrorists) employ the techniques of murder and violence to prove their point of view.

One ought not to lose eternal life for the sake of pursuing justice through violence on this earth. This unjust situation was meant as a trial from God to test human's resolve to triumph over violence through God's peace.

"Terrorism" is a label given by authorities to their disobedient and angry opponents who are determined to prove them murderous to their loyal followers.

The rise of authoritarian rulers and the rise of terrorists is a manifestation of the desire to win people's favor and to dissuade people from believing that one party is righteous and the other is evil. It is a product of the human desire to win the favor of people and a manifestation of the human failure to win the favor of God, who favors only those who are peaceful.

The authorities wish to establish their respect and obedience in the sight of their followers and the general population. The terrorists struggle to expose those rulers' mistreatment of the population. They expose police brutality, the use of military force against civilians, and the use of the judiciary to silence their opponents. Terrorists consider those authorities as non-representative. Consequently, the terrorists refuse to submit to the authorities.

The authorities, and the small number of elites who support the authorities, control the media, which in turn is used to convince their audiences that terrorists commit heinous violent crimes that warrant borrowing money, at the expense of the people's good, to buy weapons and to pay for armed campaigns to kill the terrorists.

Idolatry has produced the most intellectually and spiritually bankrupt class of leaders who mismanage every aspect of life, whether urban, agricultural, industrial, financial, or political.

Current global leadership maintains the lie that there are not enough resources for all of the earth's inhabitants. These leaders do so to cover up for their incompetence in planning for the living needs of all people. As such, the one billion wealthy succumb to their leaders' deceptions for fear of losing their comfortable social status.

Furthermore, the richest one billion of the earth's population are in a position of unprecedented control of technology that enables them to stamp out any criticism and to live seemingly comfortable lives.

Those Westerners who declare themselves to be living in democracies are held liable in the eyes of the planet's poorest populations for supporting authorities that send military airplanes to drop tons of explosives on poor people's tents in the slums and the mountains.

One billion people is quite a large number to suppress the grievances of the remaining six billion. It is no surprise that those who lack representation and those who cannot live any longer under the prevalent deceptions mount rebellions against the authorities.

Do you wonder why terrorists target transportation technology?

Transportation technology represents one of the luxuries that the richest population enjoys and takes for granted. If you belong to the one billion, you can pay a few hundred dollars to travel across oceans from one continent to another. But if you are one of the poorest six billion, you have to go into debt to raise some twenty thousand dollars to pay for a human trafficker to smuggle you to Europe on board a broken and crowded boat with the almost certain chance of death.

Do you see the irony? If you are poor, you pay more for high-risk trips; but if you are rich, you pay less for luxurious minimum-risk trips.

Similarly, only if you are a media mogul or an influential person are you accorded the privilege of criticizing. This relationship between wealth and the capacity to criticize mimics the relationship between the U.S. and the rest of the world.

Younger generations shy away from politics and concentrate on making money because they realize that politicians do not have the capacity to change anything even if they want to. They have furthermore inherited the belief that only through financial gain will they afford to have the freedom of speech.

If that is the situation in the West, a part of the world that exalts liberty, can you imagine how much worse the situation is in the rest of the world? How many times have you been punished at work for expressing your opinions? How many times have you suppressed your opinions out of fear of punishment or mistreatment?

Freedom of speech, as a constitutional right, cannot be enforced unless a person has the financial capacity to hire lawyers to advocate their case in courts of law, where it can potentially take years to resolve such disputes.

We attempt to punish critical individuals because society emphasizes a person's reputation and consequently the person's public opinion.

If we learn to publicly debate and criticize, disputes might not lead to murder, as we currently see on the news.

If we adopt the example of Christ in triumphing over the desire to avenge injury to one's dignity, the world would triumph over the negative impact of idolatry.

Those leaders that stir up the conditions for terrorism exploit the availability of a continuous supply of human beings who socially and financially benefit from their rule to drive them to wars against those who are labeled "terrorists."

The cost to the population of this non-representative leadership's decision to launch a war on terrorism has increased the national debt, which in turn burdens the larger population. Only the class supporting military rule is the direct beneficiary of those loans.

Another problem of leadership that contributes to terrorism is that society's elites are often people who maintain bank accounts and residences in Western countries and are the first to flee the country in troubled times. They leave behind those burdened with the debts borrowed under their military leadership. Consequently the weight of debt aggravates the social situation and causes more people to carry out violence against the system and further terrorism.

Yet one more problem of modern leadership that contributes to terrorism is that the followers of the world's various religions often fall into the trap of asserting the superiority of their religion over another religion. Even the disciples of Jesus fell into that temptation when they debated among themselves who was the greatest. It is another form of idolatry, the excessive adoration of one's doctrine or belief, that causes religious sects to kill one another over disputes over doctrines despite the violation of the commandment "thou shalt not kill."

People who worship doctrinal supremacy (an idol) collaborate with the economic powers that trade in weapons to prove that one civilization is greater than another. America, which claims to be Christian, is the anti-thesis of Jesus Christ's instruction that those who follow him must give up their material wealth. America worships the idol of building a glorious civilization that employs Christianity as much as the Roman Empire did to maintain its civilization. The end result of this idol worship is a civilization plagued with the consumption of drugs and alcohol and modern forms of slavery involving the sex trade and economic exploitation. In every case that humankind worshipped idols the result has been spiritual death.

One more aspect that contributes to the rise of terrorism is the weapons industry. The regions that are plagued with terrorism are so impoverished that they lack the technology to manufacture weapons. Yet weapons are abundant in these regions. One has to ask, "Where do these weapons come from?" and "Where do the funds to purchase weapons derive from?"

The countries capable of producing weapons are the same ones leading the negotiations between the fighting factions in this region. The West, Russia, and China are all brokers in the peace negotiations with all the fighting factions, while they also supply weapons to the same factions. This aspect of world politics demonstrates that terrorism is only a negative by-product of the non-representative leadership of all the involved countries. The citizens of those countries do not desire war nor do they desire to supply fighting factions with weapons.

The non-representative leadership has failed in its role of establishing successful dispute resolution mechanisms because of its interest in profits from weapons sales commissions. The world's despotic systems rely heavily on military power. The people who serve in the military are often from the poorest sector of society because the elites do not wish to sacrifice their lives in battle against their opponents. The elites only occupy leadership positions to stay in control of the soldiers. This scenario of military control does not work perfectly. Eventually the soldiers stage a military coup, similar to what has happened in most African countries, and become the masters of their former elites.

The weapons industry seems to be the only benefactor of the current War on Terror because for the past three decades the number of civilians who have joined terrorist groups has increased. Three decades ago the number of terrorists were in the hundreds but today the Islamic State (IS) in Syria comprises millions of people. Every time the Western media claim that the air campaigns have destroyed terrorist locations, the alternative media show images of women and children in torn-out buildings either dead or injured. The number of injured civilians are constantly rising and prompting the population to join the rebels. The weapons industry has turned into an idol (an activity beyond public criticism and reason) that drives political decisions to inflict death on the population.

The justification for the War on Terror is not credible. The only reason politicians are peddling this claim to the population is probably the high commissions paid by weapons manufacturers to get taxpayers to bear the costs of manufacturing weapons that only bring material profit to the weapons industry. The War on Terror is an idol (a false image) used as a smokescreen for profit by the weapons industry. It is an idol that brings death to humankind.

Case Study: Egypt's Failure

The Islamic movements failed in 2013 to win local and worldwide support because their doctrines would take away the individual freedom to question, criticize and reject their religion, the founder of their religion, or to reject the imposition of their religious laws on social life.

The Islamic movements also failed because of their entrapment in doctrinal disputes in which they ridiculed those who follow the Bible under the claim that the current Biblical text has been falsified. This doctrinal ridicule of Christians and Jews caused the loss of interfaith love and respect, with these two religious groups becoming the most likely supporters of moral principles in society.

Islamist movements do not appreciate the concept of "love". Without love there can be no peaceful way for humans to live together and cannot achieve justice. Without love, humans resort to military warfare to settle their disputes only to discover that war breeds more hatred and more division among human beings.

Egypt was a demonstration of this worldwide loss of sympathy toward the Islamists. The world supported the military overthrow of the Islamist president because it feared the angry rhetoric about establishing justice by military jihad.

The desire to enforce obedience to authority has diminished the leadership's attendance to the living needs of the citizens of Egypt. They instead encourage people to emigrate out of Egypt because there are no plans designed to meet their living needs. How could those rejected people take pride in obedience to an authority that treats them as human garbage?

The culture of Egypt is notoriously intolerant of criticism. Accusations of demon possession on the Christian Coptic side and accusations of mental illness on the secular and Muslim side of Egyptian culture are widely used to suppress criticism. The absence of any secular discourse on the negative consequences of idolatry leads Egyptians to revert to ancient interpretations of religious texts rather than deal with reality.

Idolatry in Egypt is not only the cause of terrorism, but also the cause of the conversion of Coptic girls to Islam. How?

The Coptic Church's irrational approach to religion caused a number of youth to convert to Islam in protest of the hierarchy's demand for obedience to the church.

In the two years between the toppling of the Mubarak government in 2011 and the ousting of the Islamist president in 2013, there was plenty of public news about Coptic girls who were mistreated by the church for declaring their desire to convert to Islam. An example of such a story can be found in an Arabic video, posted on YouTube, in which a young woman describes her years-long ordeal of mistreatment by her family and by Coptic priests who attempted to dissuade her by accusing her of demon possession and subjecting her to irrational procedures (https://www.youtube.com/watch?v=IMdMjmNfuUk).

Some Coptic girls were detained (often having been kidnapped or coerced) in houses and subjected to the process of exorcism for their desire to convert to Islam. Kidnapping in Egypt is practiced not only by the security apparatus dealing with political opposition but also by ordinary families on their underage children who disobey the dictates of their religious tradition. It is a cultural problem.

Demon possession is the Coptic Church's interpretation of the desire to convert to Islam. The public stories of Coptic girls' conversions to Islam created significant political embarrassment for the Church and were perhaps one of the reasons the church supported the military coup that ousted the Islamist president. The church did not want this kind of debate in a Muslim society interfering with its doctrine.

In another video, a former Coptic priest who converted to Islam tells of his experiences related to the concept of the blood and body of Christ; after taking the bread and wine in his car to give to a patient, the former went rotten (as bread would) and he had to throw it in the garbage. (This video is viewable at https://www.youtube.com/watch?v=5QR2CKO9skI.) This incident prompted him to question the literal interpretation of the Coptic Church that the bread and wine transforms into the body and blood of Christ.

How could the body of Christ rot with fungus?! The literal interpretation of the Coptic Church proved to be an idol worship that did not survive the experience of rational individuals. The idolatrous practices of the Coptic Orthodox Church are the primary cause of conversion to Islam in Egypt among the youth of the country.

In recent decades it has become obvious that the Coptic Church is losing its children to many forces; one is conversion to Islam, another is rejection of faith (atheism). Many of those who have remained Christian have converted to various other sects (Protestant and Catholic). The Church is losing its members because it has spent its energy creating an idol; namely the persecution of Christians in Egypt. It is similar to the Pharaoh in Egypt, who created an idol in relation to the population, namely fear of Jewish population growth. Both fears were defeated by God's plan. The Jews in Pharaonic Egypt multiplied and the Copts in modern Egypt deserted the Church. Both show that societies that build idols (deceptive ideas) produce destructive results for those who created the idols.

Oppressive cultures such as Egypt's create young people who suffer under the abuse of authority but are determined to be martyrs so as to liberate themselves because they have learned of no other way to escape from their oppression. The more that they are assaulted for their desire to break free, the more they become convinced of their cause. Once they are convinced of the necessity of martyrdom, they become easy recruits for terrorist organizations against the West.

The West does not understand that idolatry created them. The West does not care to debate a remedy to the problem of terrorism, or to combat the idolatry (of worshipping the authority) that created it. The only plan the West currently has is to wipe out terrorists with guns faster than the rate at which oppression and idolatry are producing them.

The absence of any secular discourse on the negative consequences of idolatry causes Egyptians to turn to ancient interpretations of religious texts and traditions to deal with their oppressive reality. Egyptian society is the largest example of idolatry in the world today even though it overwhelmingly professes a belief in monotheism.

It is not surprising that rebellions continue to erupt in this culture of Egyptian idolatry. It is not surprising that the world's most wanted terrorists are of Egyptian origin, such as Ayman al-Zawahiri, an eye surgeon and Al-Qaida leader who took over after Osama Bin Laden's death.

The title of Gilles Kepel's book, *Muslim Extremism in Egypt: The Prophet and Pharaoh,* [12] reflects the sentiment of a population lingering under a style of authority that produced such extremists as those who assassinated President Sadat in 1981. They imagined themselves to have killed the Pharaoh.

The Pharaoh is still a term in use to express popular sentiment toward the style of contemporary authority in Egypt, and is not limited to referring to ancient Egyptian civilization. Abuse of authority is not limited to threatening the safety of critics of the government, but often extends to threatening the safety of the opposition's immediate as well as extended family.

The result of this Egyptian culture of idolatry is an education system that is ranked near the bottom by international standards, a culture that stresses obedience to authority over any other consideration and an unstable society.

Egyptian politics are driven by fear. After the toppling of the Islamist president, Egyptian politics became predicated on the fear of terrorism—that is, fear that the failure of the current military government would lead to a situation similar to that found in Syria and Iraq, where international forces as well inter-factional fighting among Islamists would destroy Egypt.

A culture of fear is a reflection of idolatry, whereas true love (God's love) is peaceful and promotes a healthy culture. The failure of Egyptian leadership to provide a model of governance by love instead of by military might has led to the failure of Egypt. Love, not revolution, is what Egypt needs. It is God's love that can open Egyptians to listening to one another without fear of civil violence or military intervention from the outside world.

If humanity were to promote God's love and the avoidance of

idolatry then we could achieve a peaceful future through love rather than through military intervention. Humankind needs leaders who know that God's love is more powerful than any military. The first step of leadership in demonstrating God's love is raising awareness of the dangers of idolatry and heightening the level of individual and family responsibility to avoid this fatal attraction to worshipping idols. It is through God's love, in spirit and truth, that human beings can love one another.

The military rulers and their circles of elites in all third-world countries are often people who have homes, properties, and bank accounts in every Western country. They steal the wealth of their impoverished people to establish themselves comfortably in Western countries. The West provides a safe haven to those who enforce the idolatry that violates the populations of the Third World.

Do you understand now why the culture of Western elites has been gradually shifting in the past few decades from reason and science to idolatry?

Popular thinking makes people believe that in the course of human evolution third-world countries will gradually join the civilized world. However, reality suggests the opposite. The malaise of servitude to human desires and authority (idolatry) is a mindset that is expanding beyond the geographic borders of the Third World. It is manifested in the worldwide degradation of democratic institutions, the abandonment of the Age of Reason and its replacement with complacency to the authority of money and power.

There is a trend of affluent elites moving out of the Third World to the West, coupled with an influx of suffering refugees seeking protection in the West. Both the oppressors and the oppressed are moving to the West for different reasons. The oppressors move to enjoy the freedom offered by the West and the oppressed move to escape the suffering they endured under the authorities in their countries of birth. Both the oppressor and the oppressed seek escape from idolatry. The West does not help them find the solution in their native countries because the West not only fails to identify the problem correctly as idolatry but also enforces the idolatry by supplying the military with equipment, further empowering the rulers of third-world countries. The malaise of idolatry spreads throughout the world because it has not been correctly identified and remedied by the power of reason where it originated.

The terrorist enterprise is failing not so much due to the world's hatred of a moral society or the military superiority of its opponents as to its status as an idolatrous venture.

Illegal Immigration

Illegal immigration is the scapegoat that many people blame for the rise of terrorism. What is the cause of illegal immigration? Do illegal immigrants deserve this blame?

Let me continue with the example of Egypt. After the July 2013 military coup in Egypt, the government-sponsored media went on campaigns to tell average Egyptians to migrate to some other country because Egypt was not able to provide the minimum requirements for their living needs. Millions in major urban centers in Egypt live in unplanned primitive habitats without any infrastructure such as electricity, drinking water, and sanitation. According to official statistics, more than one million people live in these conditions.

On the other side of the sea, as described by the BBC news report "Why is there a crisis in Calais?" [13], the UK government was frustrated by thousands of immigrants' attempts to cross the English Channel via a freight train to Britain. The migrants took the life-threatening risk of hopping over the Eurotunnel's reinforced fence in Calais. Then in some instances they grabbed hold of a train as it went by, a behavior that led to numerous deaths.

African migrants have to take other life-threatening risks by sea in order to reach European soil. On August 5, 2015, a news item from Reuters, "Migrant boat capsizes in Mediterranean, at least 25 dead" [14], described an incident of a boat packed with 700 migrants that capsized in the Mediterranean Sea. Twenty-five bodies were recovered. The article noted that the Mediterranean Sea has become the world's most deadly border area for migrants. More than 2,000 died in the first seven months of 2015.

Where is the world leadership in the face of this human tragedy? Where are the intellectuals to represent those at risk? Is there anyone to defend the flight of the oppressed? Or have we all become intoxicated with the idolatry of worshipping Baal? Baal is no longer the ancient Babylonian statue the Israelites once worshipped; rather, it is the power of authority in our contemporary times. On the one hand, a country such as Egypt tells its people that it cannot tolerate them, and on the other hand, the West shuts its gates in front of them. What do you think those migrants should do? Which leadership is to be blamed for this system that caused their suffering and death? This tragic situation subjects more people to the throes of terrorism.

If global leaders understood that the problem of illegal migrants is caused by idolatry, then they would spend their resources liberating the individual from worship of power and authority, instead of spending millions of dollars on security measures, as France and Britain recently did, in August 2015 [15]. France and Britain assigned a budget of 15 million Euros for security measures to keep migrants away, as if they were dangerous animals, instead of investing in human development to care for the living needs of those migrants.

During the first weekend of September 2015, the spectacular news of European sympathy toward the suffering of refugees came as a surprise even to their political leadership. The news unfolded over the flight of thousands of refugees who departed from Syria and several African countries by crossing the Mediterranean from Turkey to Greece, then traveled by land to Germany, passing through Macedonia, Serbia, Hungary, and Austria. Protestors in major cities in Europe came out on September 5, 2015 in solidarity with the refugees. The determination of those peaceful civilians to challenge the world's status quo awakened leaders to their complacency to inaction and support for military rulers in the Middle East.

An editorial in the *New York Times* on September 4, 2015, titled "Exodus of Syrians Highlights Political Failure of the West" [16], acknowledged the failure of Western leadership as the cause of the latest explosion of the refugee crisis. It notes, "The migrant crisis in Europe is essentially self-inflicted. Had European countries sought serious solutions to political conflicts like the one in Syria, and dedicated enough time and resources to humanitarian assistance abroad, Europe would not be in this position today" [18]

Illegal immigration is a challenge that the world will have to deal with in the next few decades. In April 2015 the Qatari network Aljazeera published a documentary in the Arabic language entitled *The Black Box: Illegal Immigration* [17]. Had the leaders of the world viewed this documentary they would have been better prepared to deal with the situation instead of waiting until it erupted in September 2015.

LEADERSHIP

In every election people dream of a leader who can return the country to consensus building, compassion and fairness. One has to ask: Did not God instruct people to be compassionate and fair far better than any human being? Why are people abandoning God as leader and seeking leaders among human beings? Can human beings become more capable leaders than God in enforcing ideals?

We mistakenly believe that human leadership is capable of moving the visible mechanisms of governing society, whereas God, who is invisible to the eye, cannot.

The result of this false premise is the structural failure of societies, toward which people turn a blind eye in pursuit of their idolatry in worshipping human leadership.

Has there been any human leadership in the history of humankind that has achieved justice, peace, or compassion? The empirical (scientific) evidence from the history of humankind tells us that human leadership has always fallen into the trap of fame and power, murdering its opponents to achieve its goals. Why then do we continue to believe against all scientific evidence that human leadership can achieve a paradise of justice and compassion on earth? The answer is idolatry. The result of this idolatry is that we are continuously generating classes of super-rich elites that rule over us while plunging our societies into debt, war, and servitude. People love this servitude.

Some people love watching their idols' life stories, scandals and family affairs on the news while they live under servitude and debt. They love listening to their leadership speeches that pump up adrenaline in their systems to go to war against their opponents instead of listening to God's instruction that "thou shalt not kill."

Trusting in God is not the result of unqualified faith, rather it is the rational conclusion arrived at by evaluating the empirical evidence from the history of humankind as well as the result of self-respect and the desire for liberty from servitude to other human beings.

God is the only leader who is capable of pulling together the strings of the visible world to achieve the best outcome for every individual. If one were to trust and accept God's will instead of seeking any other form of idolatry then one would land better results in life.

The problem with us is the desire for things to happen on our own terms and our own timing. When we do not fulfill our desires on our own terms we seek human leaders that promise to achieve our desires, but in the end, even if they do as we desired, we end up with structural failures in our societies whose damage far outweighs the benefits of what we desired.

Just because I believe that God is the only leader does not mean that I advocate a total removal of worldly governments. I believe in direct democracy, as I will explain later, in the chapter titled "What is the Solution?"

The claims of governments to protect their citizens have been exposed. Modern societies, due to their worship of authority and money, have lost their desire to represent the needs of their citizens. Security measures and military spending are only driven by the financial interests of the elites who profit from those measures. In situations of war or political conflict, where there is no elitist interest in profiteering, the population is often left without any government intervention to protect civilian lives.

The political storm that follows a terrorist attack on a passenger airplane has more to do with pleasing the influential elites who profit from air travel than with the safety of the population that suffers as refugees in the war zones in which those elites are the main suppliers of weapons. Societies are caught in a process that serves the elites, whether those elites' financial interests lie in selling weapons or protecting air travel. The goal is protecting the financial safety of the elites, not protecting the lives of people.

The definition of leadership varies from one group of people to another. The most widely accepted perspective on leadership is expressed in terms of Values Based Leadership (VBL), which stresses certain key words as leadership values, such as loyalty, discipline, integrity, and service (The Journal of Values Based Leadership [18]).

Business leadership programs teach the importance of corporate values that drive an organization's success. Employees are expected to align their behavior with the values of the organization. In this leadership model, one has to ask, "Can the values of the business be different from the values of society?"

The corporate model of producing leaders is geared toward the profitability of an organization. It works well for maximizing profits. If every business is successful then the entire society prospers. This is true if and only if the outcome is representative of the population's desires and does not suppress the scientific criticism of possibly harmful impacts the business products might have on nature.

Take, for example, oil corporations that demonstrate successful business leadership in terms of maximizing business profits. During disastrous oil spills, when the outcomes are harmful to both people and nature, profitability is not beneficial to society or the environment.

It is idolatrous to obey the power of authority and money while suppressing criticism within the discipline of business leadership.

Low voter turnout in most elections in Western countries is a clear indication of a non-representative system. The electoral population does not believe the system is capable of producing representative leadership, so they discontinue voting. They are more convinced that financial means are their only guarantee of social representation.

Libertarian movements in the West have been debating the legitimacy of the government's authority and the social contract since the nineteenth century. Why?

The idolatry of worshipping the power of authority has led to a situation where Western leaders are not revered for exercising their authority in a manner that represents their people's aspirations, either in foreign or domestic political affairs.

Similarly, the judicial system has turned away from resolving disputes and evolved into a branch of the executive government by imposing punishment on those who disobey the authorities.

The problem of non-representative leadership increases as more people shy away from participating in elections. Low turnout in elections means a continued build-up of non-representative leadership and a non-representative system.

Take, for example, the Canadian Senate. Canadian senators are not elected; instead they are appointed by the Governor General on the advice of the Prime Minister. This system has created leaders who are non-representative of their constituency. They are representative, however, of the authorities that appointed them. They worship that authority that appointed them.

We do not only pay the debt bill incurred by our authorities, but many of us also sacrifice our children as soldiers for military decisions made by non-representative leadership. Those decisions are often the result of deceptive claims—such as the claim that Iraq had weapons of mass destruction—to protect our liberty.

Furthermore, the assumed social contract—to which individuals are asked to give up some of their rights in exchange for benefits—loses its appeal when society fails to include all of its members in its plans for a decent living.

The official statistics from the U.S. show that there are over three million homeless in the country. One million of those are working poor, meaning people who work full-time but the income they collect is not adequate for their cost of living.

Compare this system to Islamic idealism in a relatively poor country such as Sudan. The Islamic system dictates tithing, called "zakat" in Arabic, in which the person pays around two percent of their wealth to be distributed among the poor. This measure on top of the tax system generates a backup plan to protect every member of the society.

Over 40 percent of the population in Sudan lives on the money of the zakat because their income is classified as being under the poverty line. This system maintains the bonds of care among all members of the society.

The complaint against non-representative leadership increases the desire of Muslims to return to the system of Caliphate, an earlier model of governance in the years following the Prophet Muhammad's death. In that model, we read of leaders such as Omar, the second ruler after Muhammad, who was purported to sleep on the mosque floor without guards or gates protecting him from his own constituency. For Muslims, the fact that a leader can walk the streets like any ordinary citizen without the protection of guards or soldiers is a clear indicator of the true representation of the leader. A truly representative leader is one who is honored and protected by every person in his constituency.

How many rulers in the world today can walk safely down the streets without the protection of their guards or soldiers?

We have lost confidence in and respect for the political process and its players. A Christian would not want to be a player in a political culture that does not represent Biblical values and a Muslim would not want to participate in a political culture that does not represent Quranic values.

In pre-modern times, a person who disagreed with the values of the political system under which they were residing was more likely to immigrate so as not to associate with the guilt of leadership decisions. However in our modern times, the world is a global village out of which there is no immigration to another universe.

The current political process attracts crooks and opportunists seeking a comfortable life and secure pension, thereby culminating in a leadership that is neither respected nor trusted by the population, in either the developed or the developing world. The middle class offers a continuous supply of worshippers for the idols of politics who eventually become the leaders within this process.

The decisions of developed countries in international politics do not represent the Western population. The leaders of Third World countries are dictators oppressing their populations and fear only the military power and economic sanctions of developed countries. They fear (military and economic) power more than they observe their conscience or the reasoning capacity of their population. The result is that the wars in our current world are immoral wars. Every soldier in these wars is committing murder to fulfill the desires of non-representative leadership.

Idolatry is a state of intellectual dullness and emotional carelessness. It is a state of servitude to objects of inferior morality. A person does not care except for the worship of some idol. This behavior dulls individuals' sense of the well-being of their fellow human beings. The middle class climbs up the ladder of idolatry (worship of money and the power of authority) by seeking a higher pay and leaving the lower-paying jobs for someone else to do. The value of work is determined by its monetary reward instead of by its service to one's community. A worker wishes harm to his co-workers so as to improve his chances at promotion (climbing up the ladder). A worker fears that the availability of foreign workers minimizes his chances of earning a higher income. One billion of the earth's population controls the entertainment sector, deceiving the population and gaining the wealth and military power to oppress whoever cannot be deceived out of the remaining six billion.

Why Do We Need Leaders?

Let me differentiate between a "leader" and a "ruler." A leader is someone who helps you find your direction in life. A ruler is someone who holds authority over you.

The Book of Exodus in the Bible describes the earliest rulers only as judges in dispute resolution. Moses appointed rulers over groups of 10, 50, 100, and 1000. Their constitution was the "law" of the Old Testament. The group rulers were judges appointed to resolve disputes between people.

Dispute resolution was the main reason societies needed judge-rulers. In the example of the Israelites, God remained the only leader, who set the direction of their progress, inspired their vision, and created a new reality for the people. When people asked Samuel to appoint a leader for them, they were warned that their kings "will take your sons and make them serve with his chariots and horses and they will run in front his chariots" (1 Samuel 8:1-19).

There is no comparison between the "judge/ruler" role that Moses created and the role of "rulers" today who send policemen down the streets in armored vehicles equipped with lethal weapons to maintain law and order over their population.

Leadership is considered "a process of social influence in which a person can enlist the aid and support of others in the accomplishment of a common task." [19]

Modern theories of leadership, particularly those of Bernard Bass (1985) and James MacGregor Burns (1978), describe "transformational leaders." These modern theories fail to take into consideration the impact of authority or money on how influential a leader is in modern times. There has never been a modern state leader who influenced people without the power of authority or money. The influence that leaders of current modern states have is due to the idolatry of people who worship authority, not due to their capacity for representation.

We worship and idolize financial oligarchs, such as Warren Buffet or Andrew Carnegie, because of their wealth. However, a true leader is one without authority or money. A true leader is someone who inspires and helps you to find your direction without exercising any authority over you. As Henry Valentine Miller (an American writer who lived from 1891 to 1980) said, "The real leader has no need to lead, he is content to point the way."

Regrettably, millions engage in idol worship of leaders who set their vision and direction by the power of authority or money rather than by the power of conviction. Many leaders benefit from this loyalty to the power of authority over the nearly six billion marginalized people on earth. This is a form of idolatry in which the person becomes complacent regarding leadership decisions, without questioning the suppression of the liberty of people who raised grievances against the authority of the system.

The form of modern leadership we experience today has led only one billion of the world's seven billion inhabitants to live on $100 or more per day. The other six billion survive under varying unfavorable living conditions (Prof. Hans Rosling – Don't Panic BBC Documentary [5]).

As such, we see the rise of terrorism in which thousands of men and women actively fight against oppressive states that continue to deprive them of their fundamental needs and rights. We also inherit a world of deception, military spending, and spending on space programs while most of the earth's population lives under poverty and abject social conditions. The result of this failure is the return to what some political scientists have theorized as the clash of civilizations, a theory that people's cultural and religious identities will be the primary source of conflict in the post-Cold War world. First proposed by Samuel Huntington, the theory was further developed in his acclaimed book *The Clash of Civilizations and the Remaking of the World Order.* [20]

In response to the marginalization of a vast number of the world's population, certain social and religious groups advocate ideologies to advance their rights. For example, in Islam an increasing number of Muslims believe God is the only ruler. Many of them seek to exercise their right to self-determination by establishing an Islamic State that represents the values they want to live by. Even in New York State, in the heart of the U.S., there is a city named Islamberg that manifests this desire. The small rural hamlet was founded by Mubarak Ali Gilani, a Pakistani Sufi cleric, as a place for African-American Muslims to flee the crime, poverty, and racism of New York City. The community abides by Islamic law and maintains services to support that vision. Elsewhere in the Islamic world, you can easily find children competing to learn and memorize the entire Quran, which is considered by Muslims as the Word of God.

All of these movements indicate a strong desire among many women and men to escape from idolatry—the excessive devotion to the power of authority and falsehood, to the point of suppressing criticism—to a more truthful reality. For religious communities, the return to the core religious literature is the means of achieving the goal of escaping from idolatry.

Unlike many religious communities, the secular world has created an environment where people remain ignorant of the importance of scientific investigation and intellectual criticism as the means to escape from the idolatry of deceptions and falsehoods. The secular world does not acknowledge the concept of idolatry. It employs science in building the idols of super-rich elites, and in the media, as evident in the open secular culture in our modern cities. It might be completely unaware of the prevalence of idolatry.

One might protest: "How do you account for the rejection of science by many Christian religious fundamentalists? Science is conventionally associated with the secular realm." Christian religious fundamentalists reject science for the same reason that atheists reject belief in God. The oppressive and immoral practices of the secular world push religious fundamentalists to reject science. Equally the idolatrous practices of religious institutions drive atheists away from belief in God.

Let me give an example of how liberals' mistakes push people to the opposite side in a pattern that mimics the relationship between secularists and religionists. If you search YouTube for the title "President Obama Roasts Donald Trump At White House Correspondents' Dinner", you will retrieve two videos: one from April 2011 and another from April 2016. In both videos, Obama stands on a podium with the privilege of being the representative of his constituency, yet stoops so low as to as ridicule a member of his constituency on account of his political opposition. This mistake of Obama's reminds me of a speech delivered by Saddam Hussein on July 22, 1979 (see https://www.youtube.com/watch?v=kLUktJbp2Ug), in which he publicly shamed his opponents (whom he labeled traitors and later exiled or executed by the gun). It is true that Obama did not physically exile or execute Donald Trump (but arguably attempted to exile and execute him morally), yet the incident will remain in the minds of those who watched those two incidents as a demonstration of the liberal betrayal of the concept of representation. Obama stood at the podium that day with the privilege of being a representative of the audience. Donald Trump could not have stood up and contested the satiric ridicule that Obama hurled at him. These two incidents may have passively contributed to the success of Donald Trump not because of the audience's admiration of Trump's strategy, but because of its disgust with the Democratic Party's arrogance in abusing the power of representation.

Problems of Obedience

In discussing leadership, one has to ask: Why do people obey leaders?

Children obey their parents out of trust and lack of capacity to grasp the social reality of people. But why do adults obey?

Adults obey leaders for the same reasons as children—due to trust that their leaders will protect them in adverse situations, or due to weakness in their capacity to grasp the social reality. Adults who trust human leaders are worshipping idols. Only God should be relied upon to protect the individual from adversity.

Group pressure is an important reason that humans follow other human leaders. Group pressure is what allows a military leader, with any number of military ministers, to induce more people to follow out of collective exertion. An illustration of group pressure is captured in the popular tale titled "The Emperor's New Clothes" which was written by Hans Christian Andersen in 1837. It is a story about two weavers who promise an emperor a new suit of clothes that is invisible to those who are unfit for their position, stupid, or incompetent. The suit is imaginary. Yet people would not dare to admit that they could not see the suit.

Prior to World War II, Japan, with its culture of strong discipline and obedience, was an imperial force under the authority of an emperor, considered a god. After its military defeat this culture of Japanese obedience formed the most successful society in the world today. Perhaps this tempted the U.S. to attempt the same solution in relation to other cultures, such as Islam, in which obedience to authority is strong. However, the attempt to colonize the Muslim world, then to replace its leaders with military authority, did not bring a similar result to Japan due to the difference between the two cultures in relation to the obedience model. The Islamic world is composed of more diverse cultures and ethnicities than the Japanese population, which do not obey military authority as the Japanese did.

When is obedience a virtue and when does it become idolatry?

Obedience is a virtue if it is peaceful and if it is obedient to God only.

Jihad is not a peaceful venture; it is an idolatry of worshipping false concepts masquerading as divine instructions. Any obedience to God is peaceful.

Let's examine another aspect of obedience. Why does an abused person obey their abuser? In an earlier section, I examined the case of women who suffer sexual slavery in the heart of the Western world. Why do these women obey their abusers instead of reporting to the police? There are two factors at play: group pressure and individual fear. Both are related to idolatry. A woman who is in an abusive relationship due to group pressure is someone who obeys an idol. The group that subjected her to the abuse is worshipping false concepts that appear pleasurable where in fact they bring death. That same group of people are the product of a culture of idolatry that promotes false images of pleasure that bring death. Abusing another person is a form of desire to be worshipped. The body of any person belongs to God. People who abuse other people's bodies do not appreciate that the body belongs to God. Instead they wish to own the bodies of other people as if these bodies can become their property. In essence they wish to install themselves as gods and owners of other people's bodies.

Perhaps it easier for you to understand now why women remain with their abusers in societies ruled by tyrannical governments. Tyrannical governments are a kind of idolatry in which group pressure turns the followers of society into worshippers of authority who fail to remember that God is the only leader. This idolatry in turn manifests itself in people's attempts to control and own the bodies of the weakest members of their society. Therefore cases of physical and mental abuse of women are more acceptable in tyrannical societies than in democratic societies where people are free to criticize rather than coerced into following the dictates of human leadership. Any society in which people are submissive to political authority is without doubt a society that abuses women and the weak. It is the spirit of idolatry to attempt to own and control God's creation in the same manner as abusers allow themselves to worship (obey against reason) the political authority.

The remedy to spousal and domestic abuse is understanding the deadly consequences of idolatry (obedience to false concepts that appear pleasurable but carry death). Western societies have not been able to eliminate spousal abuse by (claims to) democracy; in reality Western cultures promote many forms of idol worship because they fail to understand that domestic abuse is derivative of idolatry. A person who worships God, the ultimate source of reason, understands that the body and soul are owned by God and that no person should attempt to own the body or soul of another by fear or attraction. The body and soul of an individual are owned by God. Any attempt to own another person's soul (through demanding obedience) or body (through sexual abuse and other forms of slavery) is a form of idolatry in which an individual attempts to install himself as god (and owner) of other individuals.

HOLLYWOOD AND
THE EMPIRE OF FICTION

We find our world today in a situation that matches the Hollywood science fiction that was envisioned back in the 1970s. In the fantasies of Star Trek, the united federation was the only civilized center of a universe plagued with wars between other savage cultures. The Star Trek was the vehicle where the ambassadors from warring factions were to meet and negotiate peace. Today the United Nations and the West are playing a similar role, where delegations from Middle Eastern countries meet to negotiate peace deals between fighting factions. The reality on the ground in the Middle East is one of savage wars managed by elites who conduct their meetings in the West.

Why are peace negotiations for Middle Eastern conflicts conducted in Western cities instead of in the location of the disputes?

The fiction of Hollywood cannot change people's behavior in reality. It only deepens their addiction to idolatry. The delegates to Western cities are not representatives but deceptive icons (idols) for their populations. People watch them attending conferences in luxury resorts in Western cities while their populace lives as squatters under military bombardment.

Did Hollywood actually prophesize the future or were the movie producers back in the 1970s preparing the population for a reality that was planned a century ago?

The empire of fiction (the Hollywood movie industry) has become the equivalent of the ancient flood that drowned those outside Noah's ark, whereas the Biblical first Commandment is the equivalent of Noah's ark that protected every living creature from the flood.

One obvious deception of the Hollywood empire of fiction is the claim that faith in God is not rational, whereas in fact faith in God is rooted in the first Biblical Commandment, which is the foundation of rationality.

In the past century Hollywood started the empire of fiction which now spreads all over the world, in every country and every culture.

Collusion of the Media

The media's collusion is manifested in its failure to independently report on the news as it happens. Often human rights organizations identify gross discrepancies between what CENTCOM (U.S. Central Command) reports in terms of the number of civilian causalities and the numerous reports other organizations independently compile. Civilians are killed by the thousands in coalition air strikes on terrorist groups, further increasing the grievances of the people in the region.

The media do not expose the errors in official war pronouncements. The public may later discover that the official pronouncements were materially false to the extent that a different course of action should have been taken had the facts been known. For example, had the claims of Iraq's possession of weapons of mass destruction been refuted, the excuse for the war on Iraq would not have existed. Yet most disregard the new information.

The media distracts people from the real problems with fictional movies about gang wars, drug lords, and an underground world. People respond to the violence of this fiction. For example, enforcing respect from others with the power of the gun is a typical theme in most action and thriller movies about Mafiosi cultures and street gang wars. In turn, this norm influences the audiences who act similarly to enforce respect from their opponents in real life.

The media produces fictional movies that portray the future of humankind as mired in war, where each person is attempting to enforce their respect from the other instead of successfully planning for the living needs of all people. We are left to believe there is no such possibility.

Instead of producing movies that project the example of Christ's triumph over the desire to avenge one's injured dignity, a triumph over idolatry, movies present fiction about such things as the *Da Vinci Code*, promoting idolatry such as the search for the Holy Grail. The media in this way exhibits an inclination toward idolatry and a dark factious future for humanity, instead of entertaining solutions to the problems of the human race.

Rather than present real images of millions who are suffering in refugee camps and under constant bombardment, the Western media broadcasts movies that keep people sedated with images of fictitious heroic battles between authorities such as the CIA, FBI, and the U.S. Marines and terrorists. Idolatry creates more disputes rather than solves any problems.

The image of the Arab as terrorist is widely distributed in the media without criticism. A recent news article on CBC, titled "France train attack: American trio describe taking down gunman" [21], relates a case of three American heroes who subdued an armed man on a train speeding across Belgium. The news article describes the man as malnourished and homeless, yet the authorities claimed that he was an Islamic extremist. The only justification for the accusation of terrorism was his ethnic background, that he was of Moroccan descent.

Some of Hollywood's science fiction movies either accurately prophesize the future or prepare women and men to accept such a future. Take, for example, the movie *Elysium*. The film takes place on both a ravaged Earth and in a luxurious space habitat called Elysium. The inhabitants of Earth have become not only a source of cheap labor for Elysium's high-tech industry but also a burden on Elysium to maintain and a threat to the way of life of the citizens of Elysium. Elysium guards its citizens' paradise from any immigration attempts by the inhabitants of the ravaged Earth.

Is not life on earth today comparable to this fiction where the West has become the heavily fortified Elysium? The stories of suffering immigrants risking their lives to cross the seas to reach the shores of Europe describe a reality that is not much different than the fiction presented in the movie *Elysium*.

If Hollywood had such insight into human reality and the future, why are movies not produced that present a solution for the living needs of seven billion people, instead of billions of dollars spent on fiction?

Critical media outlets, such as the Qatari network Aljazeera, are constantly accused of supporting terrorism. Such allegations were first launched by the administration of U.S. President George W. Bush and later by military rulers such as Egypt's after the 2013 coup over the democratically elected Islamist president.

Why are people assumed to have lost their critical analytical abilities to the extent that governments are worried about them being swayed by alternative media? There would have been no fear of Aljazeera or any other media outlet if people were encouraged to criticize. Do we have in the West a critically-minded society or have we all been intellectually tamed by the idolatry of the Western media?

BIBLE: MYTH, REVELATION OR HISTORY?

In this chapter I present my own perspective on Biblical events using my interpretation of the Biblical text. I am not a prophet. I did not receive any revelation from God. I am not attempting to write up a new religion.

Therefore you, the reader, should examine my perspective based on your convictions and knowledge. My interpretation below is only a product of my own fallible human reasoning. I am only presenting Biblical examples that support my argument that idolatry causes the failure of societies. You might want to mark with a pencil the paragraphs in which you agree with my interpretation of the Bible and note the ones that you reject, and then summarize how much you agree with my interpretation.

I write this chapter based on the premise that the Bible contains both a divine revelation and a history of humankind.

Genesis

After the death of Abel, Adam had another son, named Seth: "When Adam had lived 130 years, he had a son in his own likeness, in his own image; and he named him Seth" (Gen. 5:3). Seth's descendants in sequence, according to the Bible, were Enosh, Kenan, Mahalalel, Jared, Enoch, Methuselah, Lamech, and Noah.

If our reasoning is clouded with desire for respect, sexual pleasure, and authority, our thoughts become wicked. The images of sexual pleasure were one of the early symptoms of humankind's wickedness: "When human beings began to increase in number on the earth and daughters were born to them, the sons of God saw that the daughters of humans were beautiful, and they married any of them they chose" (Gen. 6:1-2).

Idolatry, the surrender of one's will (obedience) to deceptive images, led to the wickedness of the human race. "The Lord saw how great the wickedness of the human race had become on the earth, and that every inclination of the thoughts of the human heart was only evil all the time"

(Gen. 6:5). In the Creation story, idolatry led to certain death. Similarly, in the story of the flood, the idolatry of the human race led to certain death.

The next lesson about idolatry comes from the story of the tower of Babel, an adventure in which humankind sought to build a gigantic tower for no reason other than fame. "Come, let us build ourselves a city, with a tower that reaches to the heavens, so that we may make a name for ourselves" (Gen. 11:4). It seems that in every incident in which humankind was tempted by images or grandeur God delivered a lesson on the importance of reason over idolatry.

God created this planet with a careful design to sustain all of humankind's offspring. There has never been a reasonable fear for existence, except the one motivated by idolatry (the surrender of one's will to obedience of false images and perceptions). Humankind, in attempting to build the tower of Babel, was motivated by a false fear that "we will be scattered over the face of the whole earth" (Gen. 11:4). According to the lesson, humankind was dispersed all over the earth and languages were confused; but people still lived and thrived. This lesson proves that humankind's fear of dispersal was an idol.

In one lesson after another, from the Creation story to Cain's story, to the flood and the tower of Babel, humankind was reminded not to worship false images and to trust in God, the ultimate power of reason, who designed this planet with adequate resources for our living and instructed us after the flood to "Be fruitful and increase in number and fill the earth" (Gen. 9:1).

In each one of those Biblical events, people had direct encounters with God. The commands they received were directly from God. We, on the other hand, are reading these stories and attempting to ascertain their authenticity by interpreting events. We have an excuse for failing in the act of interpretation, whereas they had no excuse to doubt the authenticity of the message.

The next lesson in the book of Genesis comes from the story of Abraham, who had a personal experience with God that appeared to be contrary to reason. This was the experience of conceiving a child after his wife had reached an age at which it was not normally possible to become pregnant and give birth. Then, after his wish of having a son was fulfilled, he was asked by the Creator to sacrifice that son. Abraham proved that his attachment to the desire of having descendants did not supersede his trust in God's will. It was a demonstration of God's reward to those who do not worship idols (of power, fame, and prosperous children). Abraham's belief in God's promise was credited as righteousness because he trusted the Creator's power to create life: "Abraham believed the Lord, and he credited it to him as righteousness" (Gen 15:6).

Abraham had faith in God that defied human reason, yet because the instruction was communicated directly from God to Abraham it became reasonable. The promise to have a child with Sarah was not reasonable by human standards, but because it was a direct instruction from God and was communicated to Abraham, the latter took it by faith to be a reasonable promise. God is Reason. God is the word of reason, as well as love.

In the story of Sodom and Gomorrah, we find another lesson in how idolatry leads to death. The normal human function of sexuality is to multiply (produce children). The concept of homosexuality is therefore a form of idolatry (obeying images created by men but contrary to reason). In the story of Sodom and Gomorrah people are described as desirous of sexually assaulting foreigners/guests who arrive to town: "Where are the men who came to you tonight? Bring them out to us so that we can have sex with them" (Gen. 19:5).

Sodom was another lesson to humanity of the danger of idolatry where surrendering one's will to irrational images of sexuality brought death. Modern science also proved the health hazards of having sexual intercourse (whether in homosexual or heterosexual relations) through the anus, an organ whose primary function is the passage of fecal matter. The basic function of the muscles of this area (called the anal sphincter) is to constrict in order to regulate the passage of fecal matter. A person who abuses this organ in sexual relations inevitably suffers from a dysfunction in regulating their bowel movements in addition to more serious health risks. Any simple search on the web offers plenty of scientific references. Here are some examples:

- Summary facts sheet from the University of Illinois Health Center: http://www.mckinley.illinois.edu/Handouts/anal_sex.html

- WebMD.com: http://www.webmd.com/sex/anal-sex-health-concerns

Anal sex is a harmful, dysfunctional activity, yet it is practiced by some people because they hold it as an idol (a deceptive image of pleasure). It is as damaging and deadly as any other form of idolatry.

Exodus

The leaders of societies can become obsessed with ideas to the extent that an idea turns into an idol that is worshipped until it brings death upon the society.

The story of Exodus provides an example of a king (the Pharaoh of Egypt) who was obsessed with the idea that "the Israelites have become far too numerous for us. Come, we must deal shrewdly with them or they will become even more numerous and, if war breaks out, will join our enemies, fight against us and leave the country" (Exod. 1:9-10).

Idol worshiping is a deceptive venture in which the person surrenders their reasoning for an obsession with pursuing an idolized goal. God, the ultimate source of reason, rebukes such deceptions in the natural world as demonstrated in the Exodus story: "But the more they were oppressed, the more they multiplied and spread" (Exod. 1:12). The idol that Pharaoh worshipped was an unachievable idea and desire that God opposed. The empirical evidence did not convince the Pharaoh. Instead he pursued his idol worship until it brought death upon the entire society.

The story also provides an example of rejecting idolatry in the case of the midwives, whom the Pharaoh instructed to kill every male baby born to the Hebrews during childbirth. "The midwives, however, feared God and did not do what the king of Egypt had told them to do" (Exod. 1:17). The fear of God (or the adherence to reason since God is the ultimate force of reason) protected the midwives from worshipping the idolatrous desires of the Pharaoh. They liberated themselves by their fear of God instead of obeying the authorities. In our modern societies people are often exhorted, even by the leaders of religious institutions that are loyal to the authorities, to obey the authorities' instructions to go to war under all kinds of pretexts, thereby violating the commandment "thou shalt not kill."

Any perception (a perceptive image) that causes a person to fear worldly forces, such as weapons or authority, instead of fearing God, is an idol.

The fear of population growth has been one of the most deadly idols among humankind as evident in the story of Exodus. It is also evident in our contemporary societies in the frequent rise of nationalist movements that seek to expel immigrants or to revoke their citizenship. People who fall for this idol (fear of overpopulation) forget that God is the source of life. If God had wanted a child to not be born the child would not have come to life. The population of the earth is seven billion not because people have not used birth control but because God gave life to seven billion human beings. Therefore people who seek to suppress population growth are acting against the Creator who instructed Noah and his descendants to "Be fruitful and increase in number and fill the earth" (Gen. 9:1).

The claim that the current pollution and damage to nature is due to population overgrowth is also mistaken. The damage to the earth's environment is done by practices that are managed by leaders who do not represent the populations they rule. It is not the size of the population that determines the degree of environmental friendliness; rather it is the quality of the population. A small city can be a greater source of environmental pollution than a big country. A smaller population engaged in chemical and nuclear warfare can pose far greater harm to nature than a large peaceful population that does not own such weapons of mass destruction. It is the quality of the population and not its size that determines its impact on nature.

The desire to become an eloquent public speaker who convinces and leads people by mastering the techniques of body language, vocal variations and speech structure can equally be a form of idol worship that is motivated by the desire for fame and authority. True leadership and eloquent public speaking come from God as evident in the story of Moses when God instructed him to confront the Pharaoh. "Moses said to the Lord, 'Pardon your servant, Lord. I have never been eloquent, neither in the past nor since you have spoken to your servant. I am slow of speech and tongue'" (Exod. 4:10).

The power of true leadership is not acquired by practice, but rather is delegated by the ultimate leader, God, as evident in God's response to Moses: "The Lord said to him, 'Who gave human beings their mouths? Who makes them deaf or mute? Who gives them sight or makes them blind? Is it not I, the Lord? Now go; I will help you speak and will teach you what to say'" (Exod. 4:11).

Any person who seeks to become a leader of other people, without delegation from God, is engaged in idol worship, where his idol is his own desire for fame, power and money. The leadership of service and representation, where the leader is the servant and representative of the constituency rather than its ruler, is the only form of leadership that can bring peace and prosperity. All other forms of leadership bring death. Leadership by service and representation is mandated from God: "Who then is the faithful and wise servant, whom the master has put in charge of the servants in his household to give them their food at the proper time?" (Matt. 24:45).

The current model of world leadership is motivated by the desire for fame, material gain, and power. Therefore it is a form of idolatry. It is not surprising that it has brought wars, deaths and failure in modern human societies in the same manner that the Pharaoh of Egypt brought death and destruction on the population of Egypt.

The most influential public speakers are not those attractive elites in high places who are carefully groomed in the art of body language and speech structure, because the power of true inspiration in speech comes from God, not from people. Any other form of inspiration is an idol, a false pretense that ought to be avoided: "Whenever you are arrested and brought to trial, do not worry beforehand about what to say. Just say whatever is given you at the time, for it is not you speaking, but the Holy Spirit" (Mark 13:11).

The true model of leadership is demonstrated in the story of Exodus by God, who for 40 years provided guidance and food to His people: "By day the LORD went ahead of them in a pillar of cloud to guide them on their way and by night in a pillar of fire to give them light, so that they could travel by day or night. Neither the pillar of cloud by day nor the pillar of fire by night left its place in front of the people" (Exod. 13:21-22). And also: "The Israelites ate manna for forty years, until they came to a land that was settled; they ate manna until they reached the border of Canaan" (Exod. 16:35).

No person can become a leader in the same sense that God is. Therefore people ought to aspire to a model of service and representation and leave the model of leadership that sets vision and direction to God, because only God is capable of setting vision and direction. Claims of leadership courses that make people capable of setting the direction of a population's progress, inspiring its vision, and creating new realities are forms of idolatry that lead to wars and death. There is only one leader, God, whereas humans are to be servants and representatives of one another.

The Age of Reason: Life in the New Testament

"In him was life, and that life was the light of all mankind. The light shines in the darkness, and the darkness has not overcome it." (John 1:4-5)

God is the word of reason, the ultimate force of reason in the universe. God is the eternal force of reason without beginning or end. In that word of reason, life exists. But idolatry, the irrational worship of images, results in death. The light of the word of reason shines on the darkness of idolatry. Christ was the word of reason that triumphed over all forms of idolatry as a role model for humanity to follow in order to find life and to escape death that entered the world on account of idolatry.

Humankind today lives under tremendous influences of idolatry. The message of Christ's triumph over idolatry is in our midst but the world does not recognize it. Instead the world makes idols out of Christ; every sect idolizes a perspective of Christ, and fights over doctrines that have divided people into warring factions, forgetting the uniting message of Christ, namely that the word of reason triumphed over idolatry and resurrected us from death to life in a new Age of Reason. "He was in the world, and though the world was made through him, the world did not recognize him" (John 1:10).

The Age of Reason, life in the New Testament, starts by recognizing Christ's triumph over idolatry and his example to humankind in fulfilling the first commandment: "For the law was given through Moses; grace and truth came through Jesus Christ" (John 1:17). Note that I do not use the "Age of Reason" to refer to the seventeenth-century philosophical movement but instead coin this expression to refer to freedom from idolatry according to the example of Christ.

People could not understand how to fulfill the first commandment on their own. The life of Christ, who was closest to the Father, demonstrated how to fulfill the commandments. "No one has ever seen God, but the one and only Son, who is himself God and is in closest relationship with the Father, has made him known" (John 1:18).

The first triumph over idolatry appeared in Christ's birth story. King

Herod, the ruler of Judea, where the city of Bethlehem existed, was deceived by the same idolatry that infected the Pharaoh during the time of Moses. King Herod feared the birth of a new king that would usurp his authority over Judea. In his desire to maintain power and authority over people he ordered the killing of all boys (two years old and under) in a similar strategy as the Pharaoh when he ordered the midwives to kill all male babies born to the Israelites.

People who worship the idol of power and fear demographic/population growth fall into the same trap, even in our modern societies where the techniques of killing newborns have been legitimized by medically sanctioned abortion procedures.

God laughs at them. "The wicked plot against the righteous and gnash their teeth at them; but the Lord laughs at the wicked, for he knows their day is coming" (Ps. 37:12-13). Every time people attempt to curb the creation of life, the Creator defeats their plans because he gave the instruction to "be fruitful and increase in number and fill the earth" (Gen. 9:1). The solution to the problems of societies will not come from curbing creation (by abortion, birth control and various techniques). The solution to social problems will come from abandoning idolatry and accepting God's plan for humankind. It is the quality of a population, and not its size, that determines its well-being. A population that is heavily drugged by idolatry cannot sense the purpose of creation and will stomp over nature and over life while uttering false rhetoric that keeps its members blind to their murderous ways, in exactly the same manner that Herod and the Pharaoh failed to sense the murderous consequences of their idolatrous desires under the pretext of seeking economic gain and political stability.

A Voice of One Calling in the Wilderness

John the Baptist was a voice that warned the population of various forms of idolatry such as racism, which is an idea (idol) that stands beyond reason: "And do not think you can say to yourselves, 'We have Abraham as our father.' I tell you that out of these stones God can raise up children for Abraham" (Matt. 3:9).

John the Baptist reminded us that the Creator is the source of life and that it is in accepting his plans that societies can succeed. It is not by heredity. God blessed Abraham because he accepted God's will in the universe. Abraham's trust in God's words to the extent of sacrificing his promised son, Isaac, and his lack of desire for the idol of power (that could have resulted from the promise to have children as numerous as the stars), is the cause of his blessing. Equivalently, people attain God's blessing when they trust in God's words that were recorded in the Bible about Christ: "This is my Son, whom I love; with him I am well pleased" (Matt. 3:17).

The Example of Jesus in Responding to the Temptation of Idols

The story of Jesus's reasonable responses to the temptation for food, power, and wealth represents triumph over idols (perceptive images that are not real).

For the temptation for food, Jesus reasoned that "Man shall not live on bread alone, but on every word that comes from the mouth of God" (Matt. 4:4).

For the temptation to demand results on our own terms rather than on God's terms, Jesus reasoned, "Do not put the Lord your God to the test" (Matt. 4:7).

For the temptation for wealth were he to bow down before the devil, Jesus reasoned, "Worship the Lord your God, and serve him only" (Matt. 4:10), thereby drawing our attention to the act of rejecting idolatry. With every temptation he served as a role model for accepting God's will instead of following the temptation of perceptive images (idols) that are deceptive.

Some people think that Christ began a new era of salvation in which the Ten Commandments were rendered obsolete. This view is not correct. Jesus said, "Do not think that I have come to abolish the Law or the Prophets; I have not come to abolish them but to fulfill them" (Matt. 5:17). Jesus fulfilled the law (the Ten Commandments) in triumphing over idolatry. Jesus preached the importance of the Ten Commandments, saying: "Therefore anyone who sets aside one of the least of these commands and teaches others accordingly will be called least in the kingdom of heaven" (Matt. 5:19).

Social Epigenetics

One might criticize the Biblical expression that claims God to have said, "I, the Lord your God, am a jealous God, punishing the children for the sin of the parents to the third and fourth generation of those who hate me, but showing love to a thousand generations of those who love me and keep my commandments." Exodus 20:5-6

How could the sins of the parents carry their effects on the children? Is this racism?

No. Racism is a product of idol worship in which people judge each other based on false concepts of superiority. However the impact of sin on one's children has been demonstrated in modern science. The choices we take in our life can cause chemical reactions in our bodies that eventually lead to genetic mutations.

"Social epigenetics is the process by which early life experience influence chemical reactions that in turn alter the ways our genes function or are expressed" A quote from University of British Columbia website at this URL: http://earlylearning.ubc.ca/biology/social-epigenetics/

This field of study demonstrates that there is an impact on any given generation from the life experiences of their parents. Life experiences alter the chemical reactions in one's biology.

People's choices can alter their genetics. Communities that react to the same adversities with a set of common values carry genetic traits different from other communities with different experiences. If people faced adversity in life but reacted with peace and love then there is a likelihood that their children would inherit different abilities than those who reacted with anger and violence towards their adversities in life.

> *"Are you still so dull?" Jesus asked them. "Don't you see that whatever enters the mouth goes into the stomach and then out of the body? But the things that come out of a person's mouth come from the heart, and these defile them. For out of the heart come evil thoughts—murder, adultery, sexual immorality, theft, false testimony, slander. These are what defile a person; but eating with unwashed hands does not defile them." Matthew 15: 16-20*

WORSHIP

What is worship? How should one worship? Is it through religious rituals such as church prayers and communion?

> *"No one can serve two masters. Either you will hate the one and love the other, or you will be devoted to the one and despise the other. You cannot serve both God and money." Matthew 6: 24*

We live in a world where the level of individual and family happiness is determined by the amount of money in one's bank account. Money drives happiness. We also live in a world where every person's obedience is offered based on the level of money they are paid. People are extremely obedient if they are paid handsomely and are rebellious when they are underpaid. Happiness and obedience are two key words that define worship. What makes you happy and whom you obey define the meaning of worship. If a person worships God then obeying God's will and pleasing God makes the person happy. If the person worships money then his obedience and happiness are determined by the amount of money earned.

Obedience in human cultures has promoted people in their social circles because it provides a high level of satisfaction to their leaders, who in turn reward them and favor them over their peers who are disobedient.

People often find themselves persecuted in human societies due to issues of disobedience or displeasure that they caused to those who have more affluence in the society whose negative expressions might impact their reputation in ways that are not identifiable particularly at young ages; e.g. elders in religious communities can impact the reputation of young people simply by favoring some over others.

A similar argument about obedience can be made about authority. If a person worships authority then their obedience and happiness are determined by the level of obedience to their authority and their ability to suppress any criticism of that authority.

The definition of worship is different based on the target of worship—whether it is the Biblical God or some other idol.

Worshipping God as defined in John 4:23 is an activity that is done in the Spirit and in truth.

> *"Yet a time is coming and has now come when the true worshipers will worship the Father in the Spirit and in truth, for they are the kind of worshipers the Father seeks. God is spirit, and his worshipers must worship in the Spirit and in truth." John 4:23-24*

An activity of the spirit means an activity whose agent or goal is not the flesh or material gain but the spirit and eternal life respectively. Eating bread and drinking wine, as in the Christian tradition of communion, is an activity of the flesh. Loving one's enemy is an activity of the spirit in which the person triumphs over murderous desires. Fasting is an activity of the flesh, whereas giving one's extra shirt to someone who needs it is an activity of the spirit.

An activity in search of truth is an endeavor in which a person tolerates all suffering to uphold the truth. A person who sacrifices all material comfort to reject surrounding deceptions is a worshipper of truth.

Therefore worshipping God, according to the Bible, is an activity of the spirit and of truth.

Worshipping anyone other than the Biblical God is what I refer to as idol worship. It can be defined as the opposite of worshipping in spirit and truth. Worshipping idols entails surrendering one's thinking to false desires instead of engaging with truth and reason.

I was raised in the Coptic Orthodox Church of Egypt, which has cultural pride in its ancient monastic tradition and stories of saints that gave up the comforts of the world, lived in the desert, and acquired the kind of spiritual life that every person should aspire to. However, the Church used the Bible and the stories of those saints to establish a hierarchy of authority that is tightly connected to the political rulers of the country. Church members were fed deceptions of persecution by the political establishment on account of being Christian in a Muslim country. When I was young I was always told that the Pope had to praise the president, who was military general prior to becoming president, because of fear for repercussions for the Christian populace. This claim was proven a lie when the 2011 revolution in Egypt removed the president who had occupied the post for 30 years. The church leadership, in the form of the Pope, came out in support of the president. Even after the president was ousted and replaced in a democratic election by an Islamist president, the church leadership supported a military coup that exonerated the ousted president and returned to power his security apparatus, his military generals, and his political elites. It was clear that church marriage to the political authority in Egypt was not the result of fear of persecution but of desire to maintain the dictatorship.

The Coptic Church is not alone in building its politics and worship rituals based on its fear of Islam. The world nations are doing the same.

The Coptic Church's doctrine has been morally falling apart in the eyes of the church's youths, who have been converting to Islam out of disgust with the church practices more than it is out of love with Islamic teachings.

The Pharaoh killed the children of the Jews in fear of their increased strength, yet they reproduced by God's will. The Church of Egypt joined military rulers who oppressed the Islamists and tortured them to death in jails, yet the Islamist doctrine spread and their followers multiplied. In both lessons, humankind is reminded not to worship idols (such as fear of demographic growth and fear of disappearance) because God is in control of the world. God, not military rulers, would protect any minority in the midst of any majority. God allows people difficult times to demonstrate his might so that they trust in God and do not fear for their earthly existence and worship idols. God allows trials to manifest his glory. Humans need to learn to accept God's will even if it appears to contradict their desires. This acceptance of God's will is true worship of God. Fear of earthly forces is idol worship.

As he went along, he saw a man blind from birth. His disciples asked him, "Rabbi, who sinned, this man or his parents, that he was born blind?"

"Neither this man nor his parents sinned," said Jesus, "but this happened so that the works of God might be displayed in him.

John 9:1-3

Churches indoctrinate children in Sunday school classes with the concept of attaining a "spiritual height" similar to the church saints through observance of the church sacraments and obedience to church tradition. Obedience was stressed in religious literature; even if your Father were to ask you to walk on fire, you were to obey. Criticism was suppressed and any critical person was isolated.

You can guess from my way of writing that my critical perspective was not welcome. You guessed right.

This culture was not only limited to the borders of Egypt but was carried overseas by Egyptian Christians who built churches in the diaspora and ordained them under the same church hierarchy. I witnessed it here in Canada first-hand among my own extended family that happened to immigrate to Canada a few decades earlier than I did.

My critical insights were not welcome either in church or at family meetings. Worship for me did not mean fantasizing about ancient stories of saints who performed miracles or venerating idols that only please the church hierarchy but do not help me in anyway. Worship for me was, and remains, the search for the truth.

DEBATES

In this chapter, I entertain debates that seem relevant to the thesis of this book that idolatry is the cause of the failure of modern societies.

The Failure of Capitalism And Socialism

"No one can serve two masters. Either you will hate the one and love the other, or you will be devoted to the one and despise the other. You cannot serve both God and money." Luke 16:13

Capitalism created societies that built on money. People living under capitalism accepted the claim that the desire to accumulate wealth is the best motivation for innovation, competition and increased production. The reality proved that in capitalist societies money concerns overtook health concerns. People buy cheap products that they can afford and the industry produces those cheap products that carry health risks due to toxins in their content. Only the wealthy can afford purchasing safe products. To live healthy in capitalist societies you have to earn high income; but in the process of high income you work for the industry that creates the cheap toxic products in order to make higher profits.

Socialism was defined as "state capitalist monopoly" where the State controls the means of production and the decisions. Therefore unsafe products were made in socialism without people having the freedom to decide for themselves. Socialism failed too for the same reason as Capitalism; money-concerns.

Money is the antithesis of love. Societies built on money concerns failed because they drove love out of their social relations.

The only injustice that matters is the unfair actions you do to others; but not the unfair actions others do to you.

Why Revolution?

People do not find it natural that those who secured the means of living from prior generations should rule over the population whose parents did not secure adequate means of living.

An ordinary person watches media images of people dressed in suits and living in large houses conducting meetings to discuss the management of world affairs; meanwhile that ordinary person is living in modest or below average conditions. The observer compares their conditions to the images of affluent people on the media, and then reaches the conclusion that the reason for the separation between his conditions and theirs is only superficial. The rules that allow the affluent to rise to power and to maintain their wealth do not make sense. Consequently the prospect of a revolution (over the rules) comes to mind.

Proponents of the existing rules claim that Capitalism is the only system whose rewards motivate people to work harder and compete for better production. However the experience of many people has demonstrated that working harder and producing more value in work did not bring them rewards because of their political thinking that causes them to be displeasing or disobedient to the elites who administer the rules. It is clear that the rhetoric of capitalism is a deception; i.e. an idol that appears beneficial but in reality its practice brings deadly results to societies.

In every generation, the few who managed to secure control and enforce the rules that brought them wealth attempt to oppress the population that failed to secure affluence using those rules.

Humankind has not been able to come up with rules that allow all members of the earth's population to live equitably.

People are constantly exerting their creativity and efforts to build weapons for one purpose: so that the elites can enforce the rules that brought them their wealth over the population that failed to work their way out through the same rules.

This struggle within humankind separates people into followers of the rules that societies are established on and rebels against those rules. The followers are continuously rewarded for their obedience of the rules. The rebels are continuously marginalized, left to dream of a revolution.

The problem is not the impossibility of allowing all people to live comfortably. The problem is the idolatrous nature of people who do not want to help those who disobey them. The intoxication with becoming an idol is the natural progression from servitude to idolatry. A person who has served authority their entire life will eventually insist on being treated as an idol (an authority to be worshipped) when they hold a position of authority.

Peace on Earth, and the Sword

The angels sang "peace on earth to those on whom God's favour rests" (Lk. 2:14) at the time of Christ's birth. Yet other Biblical passages tell us that Christ "did not come to bring peace to earth, but a sword" (Mt. 10:34-37).

The sword in Jesus's message was apparent in his criticism and confrontation of idolatry. He criticized the authorities and was accused and condemned to crucifixion on charges of stirring public disorder and disobedience to the authorities. Rather than revolt, he triumphed over the desire to avenge one's sense of injured dignity. This explains both the sword and the peace that Christ brought to earth: the sword of criticism and the peace of triumph over idolatry without violence.

The quest for peace on earth has eluded humanity. In Christian history the ideal of brotherhood and love has turned many times into genocide and war as a result of some people's intolerance of others' criticism of religious doctrine.

The message of Jesus—who is often called the Prince of Peace in Christian literature—was often misappropriated by institutions that suppressed reason and imposed authority by the power of the sword. Christ clearly stated that "whoever loves their father or mother more than me is not worthy of me" (Mt. 10:37). Christ confronted the idolatry of appeasing authority at the expense of the truth and reason. Any person who adores his father, mother or any other figure (material or perceptive) over truth commits idolatry and is not worthy of eternal life.

Contemporary research, however, offers empirical evidence that our era, despite its failings, is perhaps the most peaceful era in history. The most prominent research of this kind is conducted by Steven Pinker. Pinker articulates his thesis in his recent book *The Better Angels of Our Nature: Why Violence Has Declined*. One of the most surprising arguments he makes is that terrorism is a tactic that is destined to self-destruct:

> *Terrorism is a tactic, not an ideology or a regime, so we will never win the "War on Terror," any more than we will achieve George W. Bush's larger goal (announced in the same post-9/11 speech)*

to "rid the world of evil." In an age of global media, there will always be an ideologue nursing a grievance somewhere who is tempted by the spectacular return on investment of terrorism—a huge windfall in fear from a trifling outlay in violence—and there will always be bands of brothers willing to risk everything for the comradeship and glory it promises. When terrorism becomes a tactic in a large insurgency, it can do tremendous damage to people and to civil life, and the hypothetical threat of nuclear terrorism (to which I will turn in the final section) gives new meaning to the word terror. But in every other circumstance history teaches, and recent events confirm, that terrorist movements carry the seeds of their own destruction. [22]

Pinker argues that the self-destructive nature of the violence of terrorism leads to its eventual demise. As the most recent confrontation with terrorism in recent decades, otherwise known as the "War on Terror," focuses on the actions of Islamic movements, I want to address the West's perception of Islamic civilization.

Pinker's argument provokes a question in the reader's mind: Which is more important, "peace" or the "sword"? This is a philosophical question that is meant to compare the complacency of authority (which entails peace) to criticism of a forceful leader. For example, would it have been better for the Israelites, exiled in Pharaoh's Egypt to have tolerated their oppression in order to maintain peace or was God justified in striking the Egyptians with plague and death (which upset the stability of the Pharaonic system) in order to liberate the Israelites from servitude to the Pharaoh?

It seems to me that the guarantee of sustainable peace is only possible when people are liberated from their servitude to idols (whether those idols are men, or doctrines or false cognitive perceptions). This liberation can only be attained through criticism, science, and reason. The oppression of six billion people, trapped in poverty, by the one billion's lust for power and wealth cannot lead to sustainable peace. Violence will continue as long as some group is oppressed. The liberation of the oppressed six billion will determine the future of peace on earth. It is conceivable that human history will not see again the level of physical violence that has plagued its past. That can only be if people are allowed to express themselves with greater freedom. Peace is not by itself an indicator of prosperity. The real indicator of prosperity is the society's capacity to liberate itself from the shackles of idolatry through free expression and critical discourse.

People might disagree about whether Islam is a religion from God or not, but they can agree on the richness of Islamic literature's concern for human morality and social order. The ideal of an Islamic society could have been a model for a successful social system. The only obstacle for that goal has historically been the doctrinal disputes within the religion and with other religions. There have always been disputes over the belief in God, and over who is a prophet of God. These disputes have prevented Islamic societies from achieving the same prosperity that secular Western societies have achieved by adopting science as the commonality that brings their populations together despite their differences in religious beliefs.

Islamic societies are consistently divided between secularists and religionists. The secularists are accused of lacking the resolve to protect civilization, of being corrupt under the influence of money, sex and power, and of being subservient to the West. The religionists are accused of destroying the unity of society with their insistence on applying religious laws to the society at large. This constant internal dispute within Islamic societies has given rise to military dictatorships that have exploited this ideological divide to rule over the population.

People can agree that a politician or a patriotic leader ought to have high moral standards but they will not all agree on narrowing those moral standards to specific religious beliefs or beliefs associated with a certain religion over another. This problem contributes to the tension within Islamic societies in which Islamists insist that a social leader must be grounded in the Islamic religion, whereas secularists accept the concept of a leader with high moral standards but without religious inclinations.

Motives for seeking justice; God's love or human ideals?

No king is saved by the size of his army; no warrior escapes by his great strength.

A horse is a vain hope for deliverance; despite all its great strength it cannot save.

But the eyes of the Lord are on those who fear him, on those whose hope is in his unfailing love,

to deliver them from death and keep them alive in famine.

Psalm 33: 16-19

There are two motives for justice; one is God's love and the other is human idealism. What is the difference?

The difference is mainly the mode of operation. If the motive for justice is God's love then the operator is God, who would ensure its success. If the motive for justice is human idealism then the operator is man, who fails because humans cannot guarantee justice for one another if they lack love towards one another. Of course for those who believe that God is only an ideal created by man then the operator is man, which is a hopeless adventure that lacks any guarantee for loving one another.

Fear the Lord, you his holy people, for those who fear him lack nothing.

The lions may grow weak and hungry, but those who seek the Lord lack no good thing.

Psalm 34: 9-10

Deism and The Age of Reason

"Deism" is a loaded term due to recent history, albeit one that is different than my set of beliefs. For although I believe in finding God through reason, I also believe in Scripture, that there are things that humanity could not have known without divine revelation, and that God is actively involved in the universe—all notions that might be incompatible with the beliefs of modern deism. Yet I cannot help but notice that the critiques raised by the eighteenth-century deists are equally valid today:

> *It can't be imputed to any defect in the light of nature that the pagan world ran into idolatry, but to their being entirely governed by priests, who pretended communication with their gods, and to have thence their revelations, which they imposed on the credulous as divine oracles. Whereas the business of the Christian dispensation was to destroy all those traditional revelations, and restore, free from all idolatry, the true primitive and natural religion implanted in mankind from the creation.*
>
> *—Matthew Tindal, Christianity as Old as the Creation (XIV)*
> *[23]*

The past few decades have witnessed a fervent growth in professing faith over reason, and in believing in miracles in favor of scientific progress. I experienced this first hand while living in a Coptic-Christian culture. I experienced people who appeared as peaceful as doves but hostile when criticism was raised about the priesthood, the church, or even the military president. I interpreted this phenomenon during my experience in Egypt as a severe case of idolatry, where the individual had turned religion, church leaders, and even military rulers into idols beyond reason and criticism.

The Failure of Atheist Philosophers

Atheism is a product of societies failure. Atheists who are happy with their friends theorize that God does not exist and that only people together can generate happiness and success. Atheists who are not happy with their cultures theorize that God must be a failure to have created such flawed reality and that humans must compete in a Darwinian struggle for survival and success. Atheism therefore only exists as long as failed societies grow. But if the person were to live in the desert, like monks, or far away from urban centers, such as farmers, the premise of a creator becomes highly plausible. It is only the flaws of societies that makes the premise for atheism plausible.

The prophets of atheism are favored by the media far more than the proponents of monotheism. Michel Onfray is an example of a contemporary French philosopher who promotes atheism and is quite a favorite figure in the media. He is famous for a book titled *Atheist Manifesto*. He also made the news headlines when he criticized Western politics for causing the terrorist attacks in France in November 2015, noting on Twitter that "Right and left sowed war against political Islam, and now they are reaping it back."

A news article on the BBC ("Paris attacks: Fury over claims by philosopher Onfray" [24]) claimed that even though Michel Onfray is scornful of Islam (as a religion) his comments were welcomed by ISIS, which made the following statement: "We accept the word of truth, even from the mouth of the worst of the miscreants."

This situation is further evidence of the impact of idolatry on the human race; people are looking for causes other than God to pin their hopes on. Religious followers have driven away those who would most likely sympathize with their political grievances because their irrational worship traditions have replaced God with idols. Atheists are driven from religion toward "rational thinking" by mistakenly assuming that belief in God is the cause of the irrationality of religion.

Idolatry means abandonment of rational thinking and suppression of criticism. It causes religious followers to become irrational and drives people away from religion to become atheists. Science, which is the best candidate for rational thinking, brings together both atheists and religious followers for the pursuit of the truth without fear of dealing with criticism and without holding on to any idols beyond the reach of criticism.

The failure of atheism lies in deceiving the public with false rhetoric that assigns the cause of their situation to factors other than God's law (such as conspiracies and politics). Atheism fails to go beyond the surface to the underlying true cause; namely that worshipping idols leads to death. There is no compromise in the first commandment. The experiment yields the same result every time humankind repeats it. Idolatry leads to death. The solution lies in understanding the concept of idolatry, then in taking action through individual choice to break from its shackles. Weapons, wars, jihad, religious doctrines, atheism, and hedonism are not part of the solution because they deceive people through false pursuits (gods). They are the tools that create the problem.

The problem is that worshipping idols leads to death. One does not need a religious doctrine to understand the problem of idolatry and the solution. Humankind only needs the message of the Bible, as summed up in Mark 12: 29-31:

> *"The most important one," answered Jesus, "is this: 'Hear, O Israel: The Lord our God, the Lord is one. Love the Lord your God with all your heart and with all your soul and with all your mind and with all your strength.' The second is this: 'Love your neighbor as yourself.' There is no commandment greater than these."*

Belief in a monotheistic God seems foolish for atheists but it is the foundation of rationality for theists.

> *"At that time Jesus said, 'I praise you, Father, Lord of heaven and earth, because you have hidden these things from the wise and learned, and revealed them to little children. Yes, Father, for this is what you were pleased to do.'" Matthew 11:25-26*

The Failure of Liberal Rhetoric

The pervasion of idolatry in modern societies caused a violent reaction from far-right movements that have been deceived by images.

Far-right movements have fallen prey to idolatry with the same force as the supporters of globalization. Far-right movements that claim to have Christian roots have not adopted the example of Christ in defeating the worship of authority with criticism instead of violence.

The liberal/secular movements have failed to curb societal violence mainly due to their failure to understand the concept of idolatry and its impact on fermenting violence. Peace was not achieved by the liberal mockery of conservative values; instead it alienated greater numbers of voters who did not agree with the open culture of idolatry that permeates liberal philosophies. Liberal rhetoric failed to find an audience mainly when it failed to weed out the culture of idolatry within society.

Humans are created to find peace only in worshipping the Creator. All forms of idolatry (such as worship of authority, money or sex) cause an imbalance in human psychology and a manifestation of violence.

Liberal rhetoric still locates deceptive and divisive practices (such as racism and nationalism) as the cause of violence, whereas the true underlying cause is idolatry. As a result liberal rhetoric has failed to generate any sustainable solution to violence and has instead caused people to become disappointed in liberalism, which is viewed as a philosophy whose rhetoric is stuck in the past century's vocabulary.

The New World Order

In 2001 the world heard the term "New World Order" pronounced by the U.S. president, George W. Bush, in retaliating against the September 11th terrorist attacks in New York. The term was not defined by its speaker or by analysts in the ensuing era.

What is the "New World Order"?

The New World Order is an era marked by the excessive zeal to prove the failure of certain religious doctrines. This zeal led the way to the world powers taking revenge against societies that believed in those religious doctrines. The world powers are determined to bring those societies to a state of utter humiliation and defeat (similar to Japan after suffering the experience of the atomic bomb in 1945). The only problem is the difference between Japan and the currently targeted societies. Japan was an imperial military superpower prior to 1945 whereas the targeted societies in the New World Order do not have any military power; their only guilt is their belief in undesirable ideologies.

The world's governments went on extensive military campaigns against terrorists starting with Afghanistan. The number of those terrorists has been increasing since that date, with the countries in a desperate struggle to defend the remains of their collapsing infrastructure. Generations that were raised to believe in certain ideological promises are not capable of easily abandoning those promises even under the might of military powers.

Countries around the world have been plunged further into debt. The populations of the world grew accustomed to the rhetoric of sacrificing their members' own needs to save their nations, whereas the rich have been enjoying the services of the poor and demanding "performance" improvements and lower costs for the services they receive.

The media intensified its empire of fiction, thereby severely damaging people's awareness of the problems that surround them and causing them to make the wrong choices.

The population is bombarded with media that promotes alcoholism as a sign of heroism, and that glorifies the culture of profanity, sex and crimes. While it neglected reality, it intensified its fiction to promote atheism, Darwinism and idol worship. The media's intensive campaigns made it appear as if the "death of God" is a reality proven by science rather than a philosophical atheist position represented by a segment of the earth's population.

One of the biggest lies of the Western political system is the claim of "freedom of the media." Freedom of the media should be measured by media representation of the population, similar to how democracy is measured by the degree of representative leadership.

The Western media is not only manipulative but its agenda is targeting the morality of the population in a damaging manner that does not represent people's values. The media takes the liberty of defaming the Catholic Church by depicting the church's history in the West as a legacy of homosexuality. The media defames Muslims and Arabs as terrorists who appear either praying in the Islamic religious tradition while participating in criminal activities (a fiction that combines prayer with murderous activities) or in degenerate (almost non-human) living conditions.

Despite freedom of the media, the media does not represent the population's values; instead it assaults its values, defames it, and promotes the fantasy that man is an animal governed by desire. The impact of these deceptions is negative for both those who enjoy this type of "entertainment" and those who abhor it. Those who accept this type of entertainment are inclined to accept sexual immorality, profanity, alcoholism and any other pattern of degradation that turns them politically sterile. Those who abhor the media are inclined to believe that the only way out is armed or high-tech struggle (as often pictured in science fiction and futuristic movies) to subvert the system.

A news report published by Reuters on December 17, 2015 provides another perspective of the New World Order. The article is titled "Special Report: The man who married Putin's daughter and then made a fortune" [25]. The report describes the reality of Russia under the rule of Putin and his entourage. Russia's elites reaped all the wealth of ordinary Russians who were terrorized by societal violence and the collapse of the law and therefore forced to flee their country after decades of anarchy.

Every fictional "entertainment" movie is a pathological parody of idol worshippers who are attempting to deceive people with images of pleasure in sexual immorality, alcoholism, profanity or other forms of idol worship that the media actively promotes. Those same actors (deceivers) who play these roles often end up dead (by drug overdose, suicide or murder).

In one story an actor who embraced Christianity described his feelings toward the TV shows he participated in by saying "I was a paid hypocrite." The news story is titled "Bearded former Two and a Half Men child star opens up about his embrace of Christianity and why he left the $350,000-per-week windfall for Jesus":

> *Jones, 20, who in 2010 became the highest paid child actor in television history at 17 netting $300,000 per episode, left the show last year at the end of the tenth season after he made controversial comments that he had embraced Christianity and found the role he was playing didn't jive well with his religious values. He made negative remarks about the series and said he wanted to exit. [26]*

There is only death and destruction in the lifestyles promoted by the empire of fiction, much as there was death for Adam and Eve in eating from the forbidden fruit. Modern societies that accept these deceptive lifestyles are failing.

In reaction to the targeted (not free) media incursions into people's liberty, an increasing number of people have fixed their minds on "principles" and learned to abandon the desire for survival or self-preservation. These principles are not always compatible with human rights. These principles represent the desire to rebel against idol worship. A person who fixes their sight on principles can sacrifice their lives without hesitation or cost-calculation to liberate themselves. Not all principles are peaceful.

Why envy idol worshippers for the deceptive appearances of comfort that they display instead of feeling sorry and praying for them?

Why feel bitter if you are poor or suffering from material discomfort? You are spiritually richer than any idol worshipper if you love them instead of attempting to avenge them.

Why seek revenge on account of any material inequality? God has rewarded you far more in the spirit than they have received in material comfort. Jihad (that allows killing others under the pretext of establishing justice) is therefore a deceptive ideology because God achieves the balance of justice. Righteous people do not kill to achieve material equity.

Why be complacent toward injustice? Speak your mind; but do not accept killing to achieve justice. Justice is meaningless without love because it becomes nothing more than feelings of anger and the desire for revenge by a skeleton covered with soft tissue soaked with hormones and loaded with desire to seek the survival of a decomposing collection of cells.

The choices we make are ours whereas the outcomes in this world are God's. Choices are the result of awareness. People who live in failed societies under deceptive doctrines lack that awareness.

Any teaching that diminishes people's awareness of the eternal purpose of life is a deceptive image (idol) seeking to dissuade people from striving toward eternal life. Teachings that permit killing in the name of God to uphold justice deceive people and cause them to worship idols (false images of piety). Any teaching that allows killing will eventually cause the rise of killers (military rulers) to the rank of elites in society, which contradicts the goal of securing eternal spiritual life because a society ruled by killers cannot raise awareness about such a life; instead it keeps the population indoctrinated to defend the earthly nation (which will eventually perish by the sword). The allure of religious teachings that depend on achieving justice in earthly societies by armed struggle disappears once the society is militarily defeated.

When military forces are used to prove the superiority of one doctrine over another the result is a holocaust that murders people because they believe in the wrong doctrine.

The "New World Order" was born in reaction to the struggle of

Muslims against dominating world powers. There is nothing spiritual in this struggle. It is an earthly blood-shedding adventure that dissuades people on both sides (Muslims and non-Muslims) from maintaining awareness of eternal spiritual life.

Economic Systems

The elites of societies in developing countries strive to live a lifestyle comparable to their peers in Western societies, whereas the common people in developing countries suffer from problems such as poverty and unemployment, whose proportions are not comparable to what is found in Western societies. This variance between Western society and developing countries in the distribution of wealth is a sign that capitalism is not a healthy system in a world that has turned into a tightly connected global village as a result of technological advances.

The disparity of income and lifestyle between the elites and the common people in the developing world leads to constant social and political instability that is the direct cause of dictatorship, state-sponsored kidnapping of dissidents, torturing of people by authorities, poverty, and degradation of people's capacity to understand concepts such as freedom and leadership.

In this economic system, the distraction of the promise of technological progress keeps people sedated from discovering the idolatry of money that is destroying their societies. Technology will not save the world. Science might save the world but not technology. The difference between the statements "science will save the world" and "technology will save the world" is that science refers to the scientific mentality of observing all phenomena, even social and economic situations. Science is the observer and arbitrator of social and economic problems, whereas technology is only a servant of political decisions. Technological advances in this century are used to fulfill the economic and political desires of idolatry. Science can be the force of criticism that corrects the situation.

I have worked for Canadian companies for which there is a growing trend of hiring offshore high-tech workers. The phenomenon is a reflection of great social dysfunction. The value of the individual's work is detached from its service to immediate society. Individuals do not sense the value that their work provides to the immediate community. Society is not a collaborative body of equal individuals, but rather a hierarchy of master-servant relations between people who do not share a common vision beyond survival.

Offshore workers are happy to be paid a higher income than is available at local companies but their labor value does not go back to their societies; instead the profits are reaped by elites in foreign countries. Those who work for foreign companies in developing countries in turn become elites of their societies because their income is higher than that of their compatriots. They mistakenly believe that their high income generates demand for services and consequently employs more people. However the jobs that are generated are of lower income and the surplus in the labor of this master-servant hierarchy goes to the foreign employer who makes millions in profits while all those at the bottom of this hierarchy of master-servant relations are paid merely to survive without purpose or long-term vision for their societies. This system creates developing societies that are without vision other than survival. Concepts of dignity, freedom, leadership and democracy diminish in light of the search for survival. People cannot pause and reflect on their values when they toil daily in jobs that exhaust their health for a chance to survive that is not guaranteed to many who fall outside the social safety network.

Offshore employees are selected for their capacity to obey and execute the instructions given to them. They are less critical and absolutely non-political. They never say "no". They graduate learning that leadership means only how to influence others (rather than convince them) and how to achieve company profits rather than community values.

This moral detachment of the individual's sense of labor value from any immediate community gives rise to television as the main player motivating a population whose members are locked in their own rooms behind screens. A society whose motivator is the images on the electronic screen can be easily deceived by fiction. Watching the electronic screen and waiting to be inspired by a song or a speech, instead of sensing the reality of your own community, is the underlying cause of social inequality and poverty.

The offshore employment model is not the cause of the problem of idolatry, in which the worship of authority and money has led to poverty and inequality; rather it is the symptom.

Income Disparity

Disparity in income divides friends. Those who grew up together find themselves divided when the person who becomes a medical doctor, for example, makes several times the income of another person who graduates with a degree in the arts. The disparity in income is the equivalent of a societal judgment that makes some people resent its valuation of people's work value.

A person who is forced to suffer in health because of poor living conditions as a consequence of poor income will become resentful and angry at society for inflicting such harm. Social judgment causes not only moral but also physical harm to the individual that will become the source of the person's hatred of social dictates.

Financial elites do not want to be judged by religious laws. Yet they judge the population that complains of inequality as "lazy": "Why don't you work and make money as the rich do?" They deceive the poor with false notions, claiming that they are lazy or lack intelligence and work ethic in contrast to the wealthy. All of these claims are false idols designed to deceive and enslave the population. The poor are no less hard working and possess no less a work ethic than the elites.

A society divided by income disparity will not be able to defend itself based on the volunteer efforts of its members. Such a society relies on the service of paid professional soldiers who harbor no moral investment in the wars they are instructed to carry out. These professional soldiers inflict harm on the human race in the war-torn areas in which they are deployed because they lack the moral values to exercise discipline toward the guns they carry and in their hometowns when they return back from active duty suffering from psychoses.

In some countries with income disparities the individual earns a different income than another person for providing the same service and is paid differently based on their financial capacity. For example, a company might pay different incomes to different people who are performing the same role based on their willingness to accept different contract conditions, and a fitness club might charge different membership fees, adjusting their charges based on customers' abilities to pay.

If the person provides a service to a poor person, he or she may offer it for free. But if the service is provided for a highly-paid medical doctor then the charge must be at the top of the range. Charging based on the customer's financial capacity would achieve a fair outcome for society instead of standardizing the charge for all customers.

Modern societies do not have laws that prohibit discrimination based on financial capacity. Poor people are forced to live in dilapidated housing and suffer various health conditions. They are not protected from this type of discrimination with regard to access to services based on their financial capacity. Modern societies only have laws to ban discrimination based on sex, race, religion and a similar list of protected grounds that do not include financial capacity.

For example, society does not protect people from hospital eviction if they cannot afford to pay the cost of their medical treatment or surgical procedure.

In such cases people can discriminate in terms of the amount of money they charge for their labor based on their customer's financial ability. For example, a plumber servicing a rich person might charge that person more than he charges a middle-class salaried employee for the same service. A dentist's or a hospital's charge to a patient should be proportional to the patient's annual income. A software developer working for a profitable client should charge higher fees than she would charge a non-profit for the same service.

Occasionally the worker who charges a rich person the same as a poor person will be treated with disrespect by the former, who considers the person to be lacking self-esteem to accept such a relatively low payment (from the perspective of the wealthy customer).

The price of merchandise can also vary based on the customer's financial capacity; the same dress could be sold for a higher price to a rich person than if sold to a person of less affluence.

Why is living in a society with income disparity a negative experience?

Societies with income disparity create a reality in which the elites steal the wealth of the poor, employ their services at rates that only maintain their survival and control the political and military decisions; those who rebel among the poor are declared terrorists and killed by the military forces that were built with the labor of the poor.

Our modern societies are no different from ancient Pharaonic Egypt that held the population as slaves for building the glory and wealth of Egypt's elites and afforded the latter enough political power to oppress the slaves by military force.

Look at the lines of people waiting to purchase lottery tickets; some of them spend tens of dollars every week for their entire life, dreaming of the day they will win the lottery. Why? The elites of modern society did not arrive at affluence by their service to society but rather by idolatry (the worship of money). Allowing affluence to be won through the lottery is a guaranteed method of breeding a population that worships money instead of one whose elites are the servants of society.

Self-Defense

Jesus Christ provided a model for what to do when you learn that someone conspired to harm you. That model assumes trust in God's will instead of fear of human conspiracies. In the following passage Jesus rebukes his disciple Peter for doubting the will of God and for being merely concerned with human fears (idols).

> *From that time on Jesus began to explain to his disciples that he must go to Jerusalem and suffer many things at the hands of the elders, the chief priests and the teachers of the law, and that he must be killed and on the third day be raised to life. Peter took him aside and began to rebuke him. "Never, Lord!" he said. "This shall never happen to you!" Jesus turned and said to Peter,*

"Get behind me, Satan! You are a stumbling block to me; you do not have in mind the concerns of God, but merely human concerns."

Matthew 16: 21-23

In the following passage of the Bible, Jesus Christ provides a model for dealing with situations of self-defense. Jesus, who was perceived by his disciples as a prophet and righteous leader, was under attack by soldiers who were executing the orders of an unjust authority. In modern societies, people would behave as Peter did and justify their reaction by citing the right to self-defense. However, Jesus presented another perspective on dealing with the unjust attacks of authority by referring to the will of God as opposed to any man-made concepts (idols).

"Put your sword back in its place," Jesus said to him, "for all who draw the sword will die by the sword. Do you think I cannot call on my Father, and he will at once put at my disposal more than twelve legions of angels? But how then would the Scriptures be fulfilled that say it must happen in this way?"

Matthew 26: 52-54

WHAT IS THE SOLUTION?

Should we strive to build a paradise on earth?

Throughout the ages human beings have tried but failed. What does that tell us?

Albert Einstein famously defined insanity as "doing the same thing over and over again and expecting different results."

Perhaps the goal of the solution needs a bit of an adjustment. It is possible that the objective of any solution is to establish something other than a paradise on earth. It is possible to secure our eternal life in a paradise that is beyond the natural world that we see. It is possible that the objective of human life on earth is to demonstrate their various capacities in triumphing over hostility and adversity by peace and love.

The universe is disposable; it is not eternal. It was created for a purpose and once its purpose is fulfilled it will be demolished by its Creator. What will remain is the eternal spirit. This is the objective of creation. I believe that the first commandment was given to humanity because of its importance to securing this eternal life. God warned Adam and Eve of death if they obeyed idols. We too are warned against following idols in pursuing images of paradise on this earth. If we do, our spirits will perish with the earth. I believe that our final objective is eternal life. Our eternity will be determined by how we react to our trials on this earth. The idea of a revolution that will transform earth into a paradise of justice can be a form of idol worship to the extent that the idea blinds a person from pursuing real paradise, namely, the eternal life of the spirit.

People are searching for an idol that can give them a sense of worthiness or safety that they did not find in their attempt to believe in God. Oftentimes people question why God allowed wars, murders, diseases and natural disasters to occur. They are not content with the answer that trials on earth are meant for a good purpose. ("We know that in all things God works for the good of those who love him" [Romans 8:28]). They complain that God allows wicked people a comfortable life on earth whereas the faithful are suffering. They are not content with God's plan for them to live for eternity as a reward for their suffering on earth. Let's say that you find yourself among a population of six billion that is targeted for suffering and death by one billion of the earth's population who are in control: What would your choice be? To kill and get killed, which eliminates you from God's plan of eternal life, or to accept God's will and die in peace, which would earn you eternal life?

On living a comfortable life on earth, people are divided. Some consider comfort in this life as a blessing from God in reward for their righteousness and others consider their persecution and suffering a blessing from God who will reward them with an afterlife. The important thing is to be content whether one is enjoying comfort on earth or whether one is suffering. Contentment with whatever God's will provides is the key to eternal life.

> *"The most important one," answered Jesus, "is this: 'Hear, O Israel: The Lord our God, the Lord is one. Love the Lord your God with all your heart and with all your soul and with all your mind and with all your strength.' The second is this: 'Love your neighbor as yourself.' There is no commandment greater than these." Mark 12:29-31*

If accepting both conditions (comfort and suffering) on earth does not seem like a rational proposition to you then why blame the Muslim world for its attempt to build a nation based on Islamic rules to establish social justice and eliminate sexual immorality, theft and drunkenness? Why are the world's nations fighting against the establishment of an Islamic state? What is the kind of threat that the envisioned Islamic state would pose to the established political system? Western elites often cite the concept of liberty as justification for fighting against the establishment of the Islamic state. Politics has become a deceptive terrain that most moral people do not want to engage in because it takes their attention away from worshipping God in the spirit and directs it toward attempting to figure out the evil desires of the leaders of a global world system of idolatry.

This does not mean that we become complacent to idolatry and refrain from supporting just causes. It only means that we live in the world but do not wage wars as the world does; as the Biblical writer Paul reminds us "for though we live in the world, we do not wage war as the world does" (2 Cor. 10:3). We strive for justice and reject complacency to idolatry but we do not wage wars in an attempt to achieve paradise on earth.

I believe that the best method to change the world is to change oneself because the world is designed only as a trial to give every individual the opportunity to change him or herself. Life on earth is a trial to ascertain our capacity to pass the test posed in Mark 12:29: "Love the lord your God and love your neighbor as yourself."

Without that opportunity, we would not learn our way to paradise. Trials are meant to happen. Changing the world is all about changing oneself (one's world) rather than about changing events and people outside of one's control. The Muslim world's desire to build a utopian puritanical society that eliminates injustice and establishes worship of a monotheistic God has constantly created wars that lead to murder and mayhem because of an attempt to change others who do not want that change and are fighting back against an ideal under the excuse that it oppresses their liberty. The lesson learned from the failure of the Islamic experience is that justice, love and worship of God cannot be accomplished by the sword or by imposing other people's notion of liberty. The purpose of life relates to choice. God did not want to take away our liberty to choose and remains in control of the outcome of every individual life because he is the God of every living being.

The solution lies in the choices we make, regardless of the outcomes that appear in the world. The choices we make are ours; the outcomes are God's.

Love

In learning about the various injustices in our modern reality, if one thinks of love before thinking of revolution, then humanity has hope for triumphing over injustice:

> *If I speak in the tongues of men or of angels, but do not have love, I am only a resounding gong or a clanging cymbal. If I have the gift of prophecy and can fathom all mysteries and all knowledge, and if I have a faith that can move mountains, but do not have love, I am nothing.*
>
> *1 Corinthians 13: 1-2*

Every family understands that love is the foundation of success for every individual. Similarly love is the solution to social problems. But what is love? I answered that question in the introduction by explaining the concept of God's love.

God's love in leadership means serving the needs of one's constituency instead of ruling over that constituency with police and military force. God's love also means having the moral courage to criticize the failures of society by peaceful means such as raising individual awareness and demonstrating the responsibility to avoid idolatry. If the individual, who is the nuclear unit of society, is loving, then the society will be loving too. If we attain a loving culture, where loving people and loving leadership are the norm, then there will be very few claims of injustice that require military intervention. This love has to be spiritual love, and truthful, instead of the sensual love that the media currently promotes through fiction.

If you love God and love your neighbor as yourself then you have the faith that allows you to move mountains:

> *"Truly I tell you, if you have faith as small as a mustard seed, you can say to this mountain, 'Move from here to there,' and it will move. Nothing will be impossible for you." Matthew 17:20-21*

Decentralization

A bigger government body means less opportunity for change.

People change all the time. Local and national elections are not adequate to enable changes in big nations because of the conflicting lobbying forces.

People abandoned participating in the process of elections because they lost trust in the efficiency of the system to bring changes and to meet the needs of the citizens.

Big corporations have supplemented the deficiencies in societal system because people's lives are directly impacted by their economic ability. Every corporation of a significant size enforces its own values and bylaws on its employees. People find themselves subjected to both the national governments and corporate rulers. This system can be replaced by a legislated system in workplaces.

I propose that society legislate caps on the highest income in any given enterprise by its ratio to the lowest income.

The owner(s) of the business would retain reasonable profits that do not exceed 10% of the business profits. Owners(s) and shareholders form a board of directors to maintain control of the company's direction and hire managers and workers. The compensation of any worker is not more than four times the income of another. This contrasts with the current system where the highest paid worker could make more than a hundred times the lowest paid worker in the same organization.

A four-tier hierarchy would consist of four working roles under the supervision of the owners/shareholders who form a board of directors. These working roles are the worker/specialist (every person in their own specialty), the manager, the director (different than the owners who form the board of directors) and the president.

The worker/specialist is the main productive force. The manager role brings a value in coordinating the work of a reasonable number of people such that the demand on his effort does not exceed eight hours per day. Every unit of work (manager and workers) is under the supervision of a director, such that the demand on the director's work also does not exceed eight hours per day. Managers and directors are selected by the board of directors every four years to carry out the vision of the board of directors (owners/shareholders).

Managers who are not reappointed after their four-year term return to work in their non-managerial positions. The board of directors elects a president from among the owners/shareholders. The president and board of directors can earn income in addition to the dividend on their capital. That income (to any member of the board of directors and the president) would not exceed four times the income of the person at the bottom of this hierarchy.

For example, if the lowest paid worker makes $30,000 per year, then the highest paid would only make $120,000 per year. All profits, after distributing dividends to owners and shareholders, are redistributed to the work force proportionately. Shareholders/owners who are not working on the board of directors receive only the dividend (10% of profits) as reward for their capital contribution. Every board member (shareholder/owner) is required to work in their supervisory capacity an equivalent number of hours per day to the lowest paid worker to qualify for receiving income in addition to their dividend.

The system would be enforced by legislation that mandates the caps on the highest work income in any given enterprise by its ratio to the lowest work income. Such legislation thereby would protect private property but also would recognize the importance of work value. Workers can buy shares in their business from their work income if that income is in fair proportion to their superiors, rather than allowing the owners of the capital to reap all excess profits.

Dispute Resolution on a Communal Scale

Imagine if we had a judge for every hundred people in every community (similar to what Moses instituted) to resolve disputes on a daily basis!

Imagine if your dispute with your boss at work were to be resolved satisfactorily within a week without a lawyer before a person in your community that you could trust! There would be no resentment that simmers until it becomes full-blown hostility.

Most disputes between people start on a small scale, such as a dispute over a piece of land or a fence on the border. It grows without resolution until it becomes an issue of existential significance in the minds of the disputants.

The success factors for any solution to confront the world problems of violence and terrorism are:

- Representation by the intelligentsia;

- Successful dispute resolution mechanisms to diffuse anger in its primordial stages through thinking, speaking, and writing;

- Successful planning to accommodate the living needs of the seven billion of the earth's inhabitants.

A system that is viewed as non-representative of the constituency will not be satisfactory to the population.

The media is also a player in leadership by providing material that represents the needs and interests of the population.

Direct Democracy – Virtual Parliaments

The main argument against direct democracy is "tyranny of the majority"—that is, populist ideas that might be discriminatory to minority rights. However, the empirical evidence runs contrary to such an argument.

Countries such as Switzerland that have direct democracy are among the most peaceful and the most respectful of the rights of minorities. In Switzerland almost every person owns a gun, yet rarely would you find incidents of violence comparable to any other country that has stricter gun legislation. This proves that the quality of the population and their perception of being represented is the major factor in dispute resolution and population satisfaction. The population of Switzerland is far more active in participating in direct democracy than that of any other Western country (where democracy is manufactured and propagandized as representative yet citizens hardly show up to vote at elections).

Imagine if for every constituency there was online access to propose, discuss, and vote on any motion that affects any of the society's decisions for that constituency. With the current technological advances, everyone could have a secure account similar to a bank account on their virtual constituency parliament. I imagine forming virtual parliaments for populations segmented by size for every 10,000 increments. For example, the first parliament chamber would be for a population of 10,000 (the equivalent of a school district). Motions that succeed within that parliament could move to the next chamber of parliament whose population would be 100,000 (the equivalent of a city). The next level of voting would be on the 1,000,000 population level (the equivalent of a province). The next level of voting after it would be on the national (or federal) level.

For the first level of virtual parliament, every person would be free to post any motion. The motion would be debated freely between members of the constituency. When a motion succeeded in garnering a majority vote, the constituency government could implement the recommendation for the local population. Only when the motion succeeded in garnering the majority vote on one level could it be elevated to the next level of parliament to be voted on. If it succeeded on the next level then the government of that level could implement it and so on. This would create representative democracy on levels equivalent to school districts, municipalities, provinces and nations.

This method would eliminate the cost of the existing parliamentary system by replacing it with a virtual parliament where every citizen directly represents himself or herself. The only cost that would remain is that of a government (executive branch such a prime minister and ministers) created to implement the outcome of the direct democracy that the virtual parliaments have enabled.

Science Will Save the World

Science has gained a bad reputation due to its association with harmful technological advances that have impacted the environment and people's health. The scientific search for a cure to cancer does not excite people about science when they are already angry at the technological advances that developed the carcinogenic substances that caused cancer in the first place. Therefore science is not credited with finding a cure but blamed for causing disease.

I make a distinction here between the reality of science, as a mentality of seeking the truth, and the abuse of science by rulers and economic interests.

The earth's population of seven billion, according to scientific research, could live comfortably on the available resources and land. There is scientific evidence that confronts the fallacy that the earth is overpopulated. One such source is a website that addresses why overpopulation is a myth (https://overpopulationisamyth.com/). Hans Rosling's statistics, which also demonstrate this point, are illustrated in a BBC documentary available online (https://www.youtube.com/watch?v=-UbmG8gtBPM). [5]

Why does the earth's population not optimally utilize the potential of this planet to eliminate poverty and wars?

Ask any child if it makes sense that people suffer and fight because of a false belief in the lack of resources and land area for the needs of seven billion people. A child, by instinct, would agree that every person alive was created for a purpose and that there are adequate resources for their living on this planet.

Ask the citizens of the earth whether they approve of the current billion-dollar spending and manpower expenses devoted to space explorations and arms manufacturing or would prefer to dedicate the same funding to urban, agricultural and industrial planning to generate adequate food supply for the entire planet. I think that Africa, under such a vision, could turn from a place of famine to a food supplier for the entire planet.

Why is science the most likely candidate to save the world? There is both beauty and certainty in scientific discipline and research.

Beauty? How could science reflect any sense of beauty?

Beauty is the attribute of any activity that brings a sensation of pleasure and deep satisfaction. There is a great sense of pleasure and satisfaction in breaking through deceptions. Scientific research allows people to break through deceptions.

I first addressed the idea of finding beauty in science in a public speech that I delivered in March 2015. You can find this speech on YouTube (https://www.youtube.com/watch?v=o9_pR9MirPE).

The field of scientific exploration and criticism attracts people's sense of pleasure and satisfaction as they discover truth. Idolatry causes people to sense pleasure and happiness in false images. It induces people to find pleasure in contradicting their opponents under the expedient pretext that there are not enough resources to meet everyone's needs. Science, on the other hand, leads people to find pleasure and happiness in devising strategies to meet the needs of those neglected by the existing authorities.

Prior to humanity's grasp of modern scientific methods there was little certainty about the accuracy of scientific measurements. Therefore, the world relied on the interpretation of religious texts to understand the world. People could not measure with certainty the planets circling in the skies so they relied on interpreting religious texts to explain the movements of the earth, the sun and the planets. People could not see the microscopic organisms and structures so they relied on religious texts to remedy their illnesses. However, you could not get many people, even in the same religious sect, to agree on one interpretation.

Since the Age of Enlightenment, science has replaced the uncertainty of religious interpretation with the certainty of scientific measurements and empirical evidence.

Similarly, humanity has the potential to solve disputes in societies and global communities through science rather than through interpretations of religious texts. Planning for the living needs of the earth's seven billion people requires more science than religion. Likewise, understanding the damaging consequences of idolatry should not remain limited to theology and the interpretation of religious texts but should encompass science.

Take, for example, the scientific revolution. I consider it a triumph over idolatry. The scientific revolution is often marked as beginning in

1543, when Nicholaus Copernicus published *De revolutionibus orbium coelestium* (*On the Revolutions of the Heavenly Spheres*) proposing the heliocentric theory of the universe.

Using religious texts to suppress the search for truth was an idolatry that evolved within institutions that professed a rejection of idolatry. The world learned that idolatry is not only a problem with non-believers, but also with the church, particularly when it suppressed criticism and scientific reasoning.

The solution today will come from science in a similar manner as when scientists welcomed the first scientific revolution, in the sixteenth century, against the idolatry of worshipping the church's authority. The world today needs a scientific revolution against the idolatry of worshipping the secular authority of contemporary world leaders.

Since people are not inclined to submit to religious authority any more than they are to secular authority, the solution will come from science, which brings people together regardless of their belief or lack of belief in God. But in religion one is likely to find disagreements among followers due to the ambiguity of religious texts.

Our solution lies in a new scientific revolution that devises plans for satisfying the living needs of all seven billion people on this planet, using the same techniques (namely criticism) of the first scientific revolution. This scientific revolution does not need guns; instead it needs intellect and spirits free from idolatry. The new scientific revolution needs to promote criticism so that every individual does not grow complacent in the face of authority, subject to the idolatry of worshipping that authority. Promoting criticism takes place through writing and speaking in a manner similar to Copernicus, Galileo and Isaac Newton, the fathers of the first scientific revolution.

The Peacemakers

> *"Blessed are the peacemakers, for they will be called children of God."*
>
> *Matthew 5:9*

The world needs more peacemakers who care about dispute resolution. Disputes are categorized as either rational or irrational. In rational disputes bargaining failures are caused by:

- Asymmetrical information about the potential costs and benefits of war.

- Agency problems, where the incentives of leaders differ from those of the populations that they represent.

Examples of irrational disputes are religious, revenge, and ethnic cleansing wars, Crusades, the Thirty Years' War (1618–1648), and the Arab-Israeli conflict. [27]

The Bible: Beyond Christianity and Islam

In this century the world witnessed the collapse of two major religious traditions that built themselves on the Biblical scriptures and the return of people to reading the Bible directly without attachment to either religious tradition.

Both Christianity and Islam are failing because they built many idols that preoccupied people's thoughts. These idols included the aspiration for leadership (such as a Caliphate in Islam or a Papacy in Christian Catholicism) that protects the religion and advances its values. Both have failed in different ways. Christianity has witnessed a gradual withdrawal from participation in organized religion whereas Islam faces a revival of armed struggle to reestablish the idealistic concept of an Islamic Caliphate.

Muslims are constantly blaming the West for its military incursions into Islamic societies (since the Crusades, through colonialism, and ending in the current "New World Order"). However Islamic societies have all of the symptoms of internal structural failure due to idolatry so that they would have collapsed on their own without the military incursions of the West.

Muslims are often torn between two idols: religious idols that lead to suppressing criticism and risk an Islamophobic reaction against them; or the political left that promotes values contrary to Islamic values (such as politically-left views on sexuality), which provides political protection from Islamophobic reactions. If Muslims embrace the political left they suffer its mood swings as happened with Syria's alliance with Russia. If they embrace the political right they complain of its scathing criticism of Muslim cultural practices.

Take, for example, the recent debate in Canada, prior to the 2015 federal elections, over the Islamic head covering, called the "niqab" in Arabic. Female sexuality in Islamic societies is idolized and protected beyond the rational function of reproduction.

Some women crave sexual attention by men and an exposed area of a woman's body can drive men into sexual lust. Muslim cultures are often accused of being replete with sexual desire because of the idolization of women's sexuality to the extent of covering every exposed skin area on women's bodies. In popular Islamic culture a woman is often compared to chocolate that ought to be protected. This view in Western culture is considered objectification of women. New converts to Islam enjoy this kind of attention (in contrast to the often neglectful culture towards women that exists within Western societies) and often express their pride in Islam as a culture that highly appreciates women. Western cultures are torn between conservatives who perceive this kind of attention to women as degrading objectification and liberals who are too indulged in idols of explicit expressions of sexuality in the media that the head covering registers on their senses as a mere exotic choice of dress.

Muslims are also often accused of using intimidation instead of conviction as a major tool for bringing people to submit to religious teachings. A recent convert to Islam might change her behavior, motivated by her desire to please more than by conviction. This explains why recent converts are more likely to wear a niqab after marrying a Muslim whereas Muslim-born women would prefer to remove the head covering when they arrive on Western soil (breathing a sigh of relief from a culturally-imposed idol).

The Canadian Conservative party wishes to ban women from wearing the niqab at certain events, whereas the political left (the NDP and the Liberals) claim to offer full freedom to Muslim women to wear the niqab. Muslims have a choice to accept the political left because it promises to protect an idol against which they cannot tolerate criticism or to accept the criticism of the niqab as a misogynist cultural practice. An article in the Globe and Mail dated March 10, 2015, titled "Niqabs 'rooted in a culture that is anti-women,' Harper says" [28], described the beginning of the controversy over the head-covering idol. For some Muslims, the niqab is part of a revered tradition that should be placed beyond the reach of criticism, whereas for others it is a symbol of oppression that deserves more criticism. These are the kinds of idols within the Islamic religion that will eventually lead to its collapse.

He answered, "'Love the Lord your God with all your heart and with all your soul and with all your strength and with all your mind'; and, 'Love your neighbor as yourself.'"

"You have answered correctly," Jesus replied. "Do this and you will live."

But he wanted to justify himself, so he asked Jesus, "And who is my neighbor?"

In reply Jesus said: "A man was going down from Jerusalem to Jericho, when he was attacked by robbers. They stripped him of his clothes, beat him and went away, leaving him half dead. A priest happened to be going down the same road, and when he saw the man, he passed by on the other side. So too, a Levite, when he came to the place and saw him, passed by on the other side. But a Samaritan, as he traveled, came where the man was; and when he saw him, he took pity on him. He went to him and bandaged his wounds, pouring on oil and wine. Then he put the man on his own donkey, brought him to an inn and took care of him. The next day he took out two denarii and gave them to the innkeeper. 'Look after him,' he said, 'and when I return, I will reimburse you for any extra expense you may have.'"

"Which of these three do you think was a neighbor to the man who fell into the hands of robbers?"

The expert in the law replied, "The one who had mercy on him."

Jesus told him, "Go and do likewise."

Luke 10:27-37

Jesus explained that a "neighbor" is any person who chooses to show mercy towards another, and not a person whose religion, national identity or ethnicity defines as one's neighbor. Likewise, one's enemy can be one's neighbor if one chooses to show mercy toward them. It is the individual's decisions and choices that make someone count as one's neighbor in the sight of God, even if the person is considered an enemy by the definition of society.

The worship of money and power in church structures has always prompted satirical commentaries. In response to the Catholic Pope's visit to the U.S. in September 2015, a commentary titled "Who's the Guy in the White Suit Next to All Those Billionaires?" [29] described a church favored by the rich and affluent who control world events, whereas the message of Christ was "I say unto you, it is easier for a camel to go through the eye of a needle, than for a rich man to enter into the kingdom of God" (Matt. 19:24). The satirical article is an indication of the desire to return to the Biblical scriptures and reject church structures.

I believe that the solution is in acknowledging God as the only leader without the desire to establish human leadership or a political brotherhood. I believe that one needs to trust in God alone. God is the most competent leader. Changes might not be visible on our own terms (of timing and conditions) but I am certain that God's changes have empirical results that people will realize in God's own time if they accept God's will.

One should not put one's hope in people or political structures. God is capable of moving all visible and invisible forces far more efficiently than any human leader or political structure can.

One of the major traumatic experiences for Muslims in the modern world is the realization of the fallacy of the assumption that being a Muslim means being a God-fearing individual.

Mercy, love and compassion are not attributes of religion. They are attributes of God and of people who fear God.

There is no meaning to saying that a particular religion is a religion of peace or mercy. There is meaning to saying that God and those who fear God are peaceful and merciful.

There is no meaning in saying that a person who was baptized in the name of Christ or a person who professed that "Muhammad is a prophet of God" will go to heaven. These claims are nothing more than idol worship. People mistakenly believe in rituals such as communion in the church or the Muslim's Friday prayer as the means to salvation.

You, the reader, understand this. If every person understood this, then there would be no problem. But elites attack this kind of logic. People fearing the displeasure of the elites agree with their rejection of this logic to gain their favor. People attack others who claim that religious identity is not from God to please their elites. In doing so, they put themselves under the yoke of the authority of their elites and kill those who speak about liberty from servitude to religious desires, making false claims for representing the ideals of mercy, love, compassion and justice.

In this book I have examined the various behavioral changes among people due to idolatry. The first behavioral change was murder to avenge one's injured dignity. Then I focused on the impact of the idolatry of worshipping authority and suppressing criticism, which led to the current crisis of terrorism. Idolatry resulted in a divided world's population of seven billion between one billion engaging in marginalizing the remaining six billion under the influence of a deceptive belief (idol) that there is not adequate resources for all. The population's wide range of reactions starts from the peaceful to the violent with varying pathological expressions in the middle of that range.

I have proposed ways to confront idolatry, including the revival of scientific criticism, the establishment of dispute-resolution mechanisms, and the creation of representative leadership. Representative cultures tolerate debate and criticism and meet people's expectations for liberty from any authority or idol.

I have stressed the importance of the individual's responsibility to peacefully triumph over the dysfunction of society. Life on earth is a short journey designed to test the individual's resolve to overcome adversities in order to earn eternal life.

I said that there should not be authority without obligation. Leadership that fails to satisfactorily represent its constituents' needs, and to resolve their disputes, eventually loses its legitimacy to exercise authority in the perception of the constituency. The idolatry of enforcing respect for authority among citizens has distracted leaders from their assumed commitment to care for the well-being of the population and has turned them into rulers punishing people with military force.

Furthermore, I have illustrated how global leaders have treated a great segment of the earth's population as if they were unwanted human garbage, and terrorist organizations have taught those labeled as such that they were created to be vicegerents of God on earth. They taught them to pray, fast, cover their bodies with veils, abstain from sexual immorality, consumption of drugs and alcohol, and fight jihad against their non-representative rulers. This created the so-called "terrorism" of today. Attempting to remedy the problem of terrorism by adding more military and police force therefore exacerbates the problem and increases the number of people harmed by the authorities.

Finally, I stressed the importance of loving without an expectation of earthly justice. It is unrealistic to expect justice from the world. The individual eternal reward is measured by their capacity to deal lovingly towards unfair treatment and injustices. Justice is about how you deal with others. If you define justice as your expectation for people to deal fairly with you then you will adjust your behavior to match other people unfair treatment of you and consequently there will be not justice for both you and others.

I demonstrated the value of criticism as a means of confronting idolatry. It is in understanding and avoiding the damaging consequences of idolatry that I hope the reader too will find the peace within that comes from breaking through its shackles, and peace with others despite living in a world full of violence. It is the first of the Ten Commandments that the human race has held sacred because of its utmost importance to empower people to form healthy society and culture. It is the recipe for living together.

And God spoke all these words:

"I am the Lord your God, who brought you out of Egypt, out of the land of slavery.

"You shall have no other gods before me.

"You shall not make for yourself an image in the form of anything in heaven above or on the earth beneath or in the waters below. You shall not bow down to them or worship them; for I, the Lord your God, am a jealous God, punishing the children for the sin of the parents to the third and fourth generation of those who hate me, but showing love to a thousand generations of those who love me and keep my commandments.

Exodus 20:1-6

BIBLIOGRAPHY

[1] https://www.youtube.com/watch?v=dfbdqVv9tiE, Director, *Slavery: A 21st Century Evil - Charcoal slaves.* [Film]. Aljazeera English, 2011.

[2] https://www.youtube.com/watch?v=arSEALgiOr4, Director, *Slavery: A 21st Century Evil - Bridal slaves.* [Film]. Aljazeera English, 2011.

[3] Chinta Puxley, CBC News, "Almost half of newborns seized in Manitoba have developmental, addiction issues," 04 10 2015. [Online]. Available: http://www.cbc.ca/news/canada/manitoba/almost-half-of-newborns-seized-in-manitoba-have-developmental-addiction-issues-1.3256137.

[4] The Associated Press , "Vatican Fires Gay Priest Who Came Out Before Global Meeting," 04 10 2015. [Online]. Available: http://www.nbcnews.com/news/religion/vatican-fires-gay-priest-who-came-out-global-meeting-n438056.

[5] *Don't Panic - Documentary - Hans Rosling is a Swedish medical doctor, academic, statistician, and public speaker. He is Professor of International Health at Karolinska Institute and co-founder and chairman of the Gapminder Foundation, which developed the.* [Film]. BBC This World https://www.youtube.com/watch?v=-UbmG8gtBPM.

[6] C. Saskatoon, "Saskatoon man gets 17 months for harassing judge," 4 August 2015. [Online]. Available: http://saskatoon.ctvnews.ca/saskatoon-man-gets-17-months-for-harassing-judge-1.2501976.

[7] The Huffington Post , "Judge Handcuffs Defense Attorney In Court To Teach Her 'A Lesson' For Speaking Out," 27 05 2016. [Online].

Available: http://www.huffingtonpost.com/entry/judge-handcuffs-defense-attorney_us_5748744ee4b0dacf7ad4bea3.

[8] J. Imam, "South Carolina officer shoots unarmed white teen during pot bust," 10 August 2015. [Online]. Available: http://www.cnn.com/2015/08/06/us/seneca-teen-dead-police-shooting/index.html.

[9] B. Graveland, "Mother of Calgary man killed in Syria calls Harper terrorism plan 'window dressing'," The Canadian Press, 10 August 2015. [Online]. Available: http://calgaryherald.com/news/politics/mother-of-calgary-man-killed-in-syria-calls-harper-terrorism-plan-window-dressing.

[10 C. NEWS, "Suspect in deadly on-air attack blamed Charleston
]   shooting," 26 August 2015. [Online]. Available: http://www.cbsnews.com/news/wdbj-shootig-suspect-vester-lee-flanagan-suspect-in-deadly-virginia-television-shooting-of-alison/.

[11 C. D. a. L. B. T. Rees Shapiro, "Slain victims of mass shooting at
]   Oregon college identified," 2 10 2015. [Online]. Available: https://www.washingtonpost.com/national/probe-in-college-slayings-peers-into-web-rants-and-possible-religious-rage/2015/10/02/d250007a-68ea-11e5-8325-a42b5a459b1e_story.html.

[12 G. Kepel, Muslim Extremism in Egypt; the Prophet and Pharaoh
]   https://archive.org/details/bub_gb_onEVLpwB7OwC, Berkeley : University of California Press, ISBN 0520239342, 1985.

[13 "Why is there a crisis in Calais?," 30 July 2015. [Online]. Available:
]   http://www.bbc.com/news/uk-29074736.

[14 P. P. a. S. Scherer, "Migrant boat capsizes in Mediterranean, at least
]   25 dead," 5 August 2015. [Online]. Availablc: http://www.reuters.com/article/2015/08/05/us-europe-migrants-

italy-idUSKCN0QA1N020150805.

[15 Associated Press, "Britain, France boost security to stop migrants
]   from Channel," 20 August 2015. [Online]. Available:
     http://www.dailymail.co.uk/wires/ap/article-3204373/Britain-
     France-boost-security-stop-migrants-Channel.html.

[16 A. BARNARD, "Exodus of Syrians Highlights Political Failure of
]   the West," 04 09 2015. [Online]. Available:
     http://www.nytimes.com/2015/09/05/world/middleeast/exodus-
     of-syrians-highlights-political-failure-of-the-west.html.

[17 Aljazeera, Director, *The Black Box: The Illegal Immigration.* [Film].
]   Aljazeera, https://www.youtube.com/watch?v=kuBzGKeaSIg,
     April 2015.

[18 J. O'TOOLE, "The Journal of Values Based Leadership JVBL,"
]   [Online]. Available:
     http://www.valuesbasedleadershipjournal.com/issues/vol1issue1/o
     toole.php.

[19 "Leadershp," [Online]. Available:
]   https://en.wikipedia.org/wiki/Leadership.

[20 S. P. Huntington, The Clash of Civilizations and the Remaking of
]   World Order, New York, Simon & Schuster, ISBN 0-684-84441-9,
     1996.

[21 T. A. P. Elaine Ganley and Maggy Donaldson, "France train attack:
]   American trio describe taking down gunman," 23 August 2015.
     [Online]. Available: http://www.cbc.ca/news/world/france-train-
     attack-american-trio-describe-taking-down-gunman-1.3200925.

[22 S. Pinker, The Better Angels of Our Nature: Why Violence Has
]   Declined, Penguin Publishing Group, 2011-10-04.

[23 M. Tindal, Christianity as Old as the Creation, London, 1730.
]

[24 BBC NEWS Hugh Schofield , "Paris attacks: Fury over claims by
] philosopher Onfray," 25 November 2015. [Online]. Available:
http://www.bbc.com/news/world-europe-34904939.

[25 Reusters: Jack Stubbs, Andrey Kuzmin, Stephen Grey and Roman
] Anin , "Special Report: The man who married Putin's daughter and
then made a fortune," 17 12 2015. [Online]. Available:
http://www.reuters.com/article/us-russia-capitalism-shamalov-
specialrep-idUSKBN0U02SF20151217.

[26 MailOnline, "Bearded former Two and a Half Men child star opens
] up about his embrace of Christianity and why he left the $350,000-
per-week windfall for Jesus," 05 01 2016. [Online]. Available:
http://www.dailymail.co.uk/news/article-2582653/I-paid-
hypocrite-Former-Two-Half-Men-star-opens-embrace-
Christianity.html.

[27 M. O. Jackson, "The Reasons for Wars" – an Updated Survey,
] Department of Economics, Stanford University, Stanford, California
http://web.stanford.edu/~jacksonm/war-overview.pdf.

[28 The Globe and Mail, "Niqabs 'rooted in a culture that is anti-
] women,' Harper says," 03 2015. [Online]. Available:
http://www.theglobeandmail.com/news/politics/niqabs-rooted-in-
a-culture-that-is-anti-women-harper-says/article23395242/.

[29 M. Winship, "Who's the Guy in the White Suit Next to All Those
] Billionaires?," 01 10 2015. [Online]. Available:
http://billmoyers.com/2015/10/01/whos-the-guy-in-the-white-
suit-next-to-all-those-billionaires/.

[30 "Motivational Leadership," Wikipedia, [Online]. Available:

]   https://en.wikipedia.org/wiki/Transformational_leadership.

[31 Human Rights Watch, "Egypt," HRW
]   https://www.hrw.org/middle-east/n-africa/egypt, [Online].
    Available: https://www.hrw.org/middle-east/n-africa/egypt.

[32 HRW, "All According to Plan," 2015. [Online]. Available:
]   https://www.hrw.org/report/2014/08/12/all-according-plan/raba-
    massacre-and-mass-killings-protesters-egypt.

[33 M. Clarke, A Study of the Role of 'Representative' Leadership in
]   Stimulating Organization Democracy
    https://dspace.lib.cranfield.ac.uk/bitstream/1826/1983/1/Role of
    Representative Leadership.pdf, SAGE Journals Online and
    HighWire Press platforms, 2006.

[34 Reuters, "Sisi makes surprise Coptic Christmas visit," 07 01 2015.
]   [Online]. Available: http://english.alarabiya.net/en/News/middle-
    east/2015/01/07/Sisi-becomes-Egypt-s-first-president-to-attend-
    Coptic-Christmas.html.

[35 E. Moussa, "My madrassa classmate hated politics. Then he joined
]   the Islamic State.," 21 09 2015. [Online]. Available:
    https://www.washingtonpost.com/opinions/my-madrassa-
    classmate-hated-politics-then-joined-the-islamic-
    state/2015/08/21/b8ebe826-4769-11e5-8e7d-
    9c033e6745d8_story.html?postshare=6581440171664676.

[36 The Sun Daily, "Leonardo DiCaprio told to change name," 01 01
]   2016. [Online]. Available:
    http://www.thesundaily.my/news/1653438.

[37 L'Esspresso, "Caso Regeni, le immagini dei bunker del Cairo dove
]   vengono torturati i prigionieri - l'Espresso," 2016. [Online].
    Available:
    http://espresso.repubblica.it/archivio/2016/04/14/news/caso-

regeni-le-immagini-dei-bunker-delle-torture-del-cairo-
1.259824?ref=HEF_RULLO.

[38 A. P. Brian Rohan, "Egypt threatens to shut down center
]   documenting torture," 2016. [Online]. Available:
      http://www.beaumontenterprise.com/news/crime/article/Egypt-
      threatens-center-documenting-torture-with-7232118.php.

[39 C. News, "Almost half of newborns seized in Manitoba have
]   developmental, addiction issues," 2014. [Online]. Available:
      http://www.cbc.ca/news/canada/manitoba/almost-half-of-
      newborns-seized-in-manitoba-have-developmental-addiction-issues-
      1.3256137.

ABOUT THE AUTHOR

The author was born in Egypt. He was raised in the Coptic Orthodox Church of Egypt for the first 26 years of life. He then immigrated to Canada in 1990. He is married and currently lives with his wife and four children in Vancouver, British Columbia. He has worked since arriving in Canada in the field of software development, engineering and architecture.

www.ingramcontent.com/pod-product-compliance
Lightning Source LLC
Chambersburg PA
CBHW051944280526
45789CB00009B/3168